ROMANTICISM

Problems of Definition, Explanation, and Evaluation

PROBLEMS IN EUROPEAN CIVILIZATION

ROMANTICISM

Problems of Definition, Explanation, and Evaluation

EDITED WITH AN INTRODUCTION BY
John B. Halsted, AMHERST COLLEGE

D. C. HEATH AND COMPANY
Lexington, Massachusetts

Table of Contents

Introduction

THE term *Romanticism* came into currency at the very beginning of the nineteenth century. The history of the terms *romance* and *romantic* can be traced, at least in their French forms, as far back as the later Middle Ages, but the word *Romanticism* came to signify a cultural phenomenon of major importance only after a group of German poets, dramatists, and critics (Tieck, Novalis, and others, led by the brothers Schlegel) gave it vague definition by reference to their works as Romantic and to themselves as the Romantic School. They also supplied the beginnings of the demarcation now so often made between their own work and that of the Enlightenment of the eighteenth century, by identifying the characteristics of modern culture with Christianity (as against an irreligious Enlightenment), indicating both a sense of their own novelty and simultaneously the ties which they felt with the Middle Ages.

Of course these artists were not so unique as they believed. The attitudes they espoused, the art forms they favored, their very distastes were not confined to Germany at the turn of the century. Europe, for all its national, geographical, and cultural divergences, had increasingly, in the preceding century, become a cosmopolitan intellectual world. Above all, it had absorbed the products of French culture, and had responded to common impressions and common events. Historians of culture have found in the early eighteenth century, in Britain and France as well as in Germany, tastes, sentiments, and philosophic attitudes which were expressed with

increasing confidence by intellectuals after 1800.

Whether these early changes should now be called Romantic, or whether Preromantic is a more suitable designation, is perhaps less significant than is the fact that new tastes and new ideas had spread. The taste for Gothic architecture and the opposition to formal gardening were early evidences of what proved to be an aesthetic and intellectual revolution. As a further example, through the course of the eighteenth century what may be called "the cult of enthusiasm" implied a revolution in moral, religious, and philosophic ideas. The successes of Wesleyan Methodism in Britain, of Pietism on the continent, and the popularity of Rousseau which extended beyond France, all indicated that a revision of traditional attitudes was in the making. The great nineteenth-century French historian Hyppolyte Taine paints a striking picture in his *Ancien Régime* of the adoption by the French upper classes before the French revolution of the new *fashion* of enthusiasm, of profound emotion expressed in weeping and swooning, of affection and admiration for the simple virtues of simple people who presumably enjoyed the spiritual benefits of rural and agricultural activity. A new view of the role of emotion can here be seen to have possessed significant political implications in its glorification of people who did not possess the advantages of wealth, education, and rank.

Such new ideas had their influence on the coming of the great social and political revolution to the Western world which began in America and found its apotheosis in France in 1789. Of course the leaders of the revolutions and the theorists of revolution depended heavily upon older ideas typical of the Enlightenment: the primacy of reason, the universality of Natural Law, mechanistic and atomistic interpretations of the Universe and of society, and faith in progress through science. But men's activities were shaped and their deeds justified also in accord with the ideas enunciated by Rousseau, the Wesleyans, the Pietists, and others. Interwoven in the hopes and aims, in the very fashions and styles of behavior of the revolutionary era, were ideas and attitudes which were formulated in opposition to the Enlightenment, for just as the *philosophes* for a century had criticised the *Old Régime,* there had for a generation existed an undercurrent of criticism of the *philosophes* themselves. Some of this latter criticism had been directed against French cultural dominance, as was the effort to create a uniquely German literature in the *Sturm und Drang* movement; some against the Enlightenment's characteristically urban emphasis; some against what was felt to be its excessive faith in reason, or its insufficient faith in faith. From whatever source the ideas arose, the events of the French Revolution, affecting almost all Europeans, and affecting them in vital areas of their existence, helped to transmit, to transform, or to formulate in new ways through imitation or opposition, the tastes, sentiments, and ideas of the eighteenth century's opposition to the Enlightenment, and to produce a revolution in thought which had earlier only been adumbrated.

Students of modern culture have long been in agreement that such significant changes occurred. It has been accepted that in the latter part of the eighteenth and the first half of the nineteenth centuries new forms, new subjects, new symbols appeared in the arts, and that religious, philosophical, political, social, and historical thought all underwent a transformation. These cultural changes reveal similarities and interconnections, and to these the term *Romanticism* has come to be applied. *Romanticism* is used to refer to this cultural, intellectual revolution as a whole or to some parts of it. The study of Romanticism has been greatly complicated because these changes accompanied the transformation of the European economy by what we call the Industrial Revolution, and the reshaping of European politics and society by the French Revolution. These revolutions are not neatly separable; they were concurrent, interwoven, and mutually influential upon one another.

The impact of industrialization upon all Europe came only after changing forms of economy and attendant social problems spread from Britain to the continent. The impact of the French Revolution came earlier and more forcefully. In the course of the French Revolution, in support of it, or in opposition to it, the revolution in thought was accelerated. Among Frenchmen, the doctrine of the sovereignty of the people, of the nation as an organic unit, the cult of revolutionary fervor, all found expression. Opponents of the Revolution such as Burke and a number of German theorists formulated new organismic doctrines which stressed tradition, the natural growth of institutions, and the power of such irrational forces as custom. Such ideas were set against what were viewed as the oversimplifications of French Enlightenment philosophy, and emanated from literature and the arts as well as from philosophy and political theory.

The influence of the ideas produced or reinforced by their revolutionary setting by no means ceased with the defeat of Napoleon or with the Restoration at the end of the Napoleonic wars. Nor did the intellectual revolution cease, much as some contemporaries of these events believed it must. The continuing change had not begun with the Revolution, nor did it depend solely upon the course of the Revolution. Certainly the formulation of social and political doctrines can be most clearly connected with the international wars of the era, and with the regicide and terror in France. But intellectual disciplines and interests changed for other reasons as well. Artists and philosophers, critics and publicists were not always at war, nor was war everywhere continuous; political and social concerns did not put an end to publication, to art exhibitions, to concerts, to universities. In each of the several intellectual and artistic fields traditions of long standing existed; forms of discipline and training had a long history. Some of the changes which occurred around the end of the eighteenth century appear to have very little direct relation to the great political events of the time. They seem to stem in part at least from the desire of the young to outdo their elders, to attain fame and recognition for themselves, to demonstrate what came to be recognized as one of the central values of the era, that of creative genius which might revolutionize all aspects of life. Yet even these objectives suggest relationships to the ideal of individuality, or to major social changes which were disrupting the old channels of advancement or forms of recognition in the arts or in the world of intellect. They serve to suggest that while some men still pursued knowledge or studied art in traditional ways, in many cases, even where the change was simply the adaptation to one discipline of ideas, forms, or techniques from another, old ways and old ideas were not enough for many artists and intellectuals. New ways and new ideas were sought which might be appropriate to the changed world, the new world emerging from the revolution. The impact upon the lives of Europeans of the French Revolution, and of the social changes and conflicting ideas which spread with it (or arose in opposition to it) opened to question all traditional forms and values; intellectuals of that period were thoroughly conscious of their revolutionary situation. With them began the controversy over Romanticism which has continued to our day.

Through the first half of the nineteenth century more and more intellectuals identified themselves as Romantics; by the 1820's there was a French Romantic School, quite different from the German, yet sharing in some of its attitudes. Among the English there was less community among intellectuals, but at least among their opponents there was agreement that a Romantic school existed.

The opinions, attitudes, and art forms, which were increasingly predominant in Europe in the first half of the nineteenth century, have colored and affected Western culture ever since, not merely in the arts, but in politics, philosophy, and religion. And hence the discussion of Romanticism has become ever more complex. In the early years of the nineteenth century the debate centered chiefly upon issues of taste and artistic criticism, the issues varying from place to place, partly as a consequence of the varying degrees of firmness with which dedication to Aristotelian and Classical artistic rules and tastes had predominated in the preceding era. And yet from the first, discussion was not consistently so restricted. For Romanticism, whatever its antecedents, and whatever precisely it is taken to be, occurred in an era of revolution, both social and political. Its definition, its explanation, and its evaluation became enmeshed in issues which engaged the most vehement partisan passions, for men felt it touched upon the most controversial aspects of existence.

The changes in the arts were not merely formal. They suggested, reflected, or affirmed changing views of the nature of humankind, of the world — both natural and social — in which it lived, and since art serves as commentary upon existence, they proposed new values, and new forms of criticism. Art critics were concerned, just as were the increasingly self-conscious artists, with the relation of art to nature, to society, and to the most fundamental problems of human existence — and hence the most complex issues of philosophy came to be involved in what in origin was a debate about what is acceptable art. Just as the artist's discussion of society was connected with current social and political ideas, so his work reflected current philosophic speculation as to the nature of the world in which man existed and the character and forms of man's knowledge thereof, and propounded new views of the phenomenon of creativity. The new concern for *genius,* for the artist as the shaper of reality (Shelley called poets "the unacknowledged legislators of the world") posed in a novel form the old issue of man's power to control his destiny. The new view of the heroic creative artist found a parallel in contemporary adulation of Napoleon as the dynamic shaper of the *political* world.

The intermixture of ideas and attitudes from various disciplines and areas of concern, and the consciousness of the intermixture on the part of many of the Romanticists themselves, helps to explain how so wide a variety of specialists have come to concern themselves with Romanticism, enhancing, as a result, the possibilities of disagreement.

The intellectuals of the Romantic era constructed a radically oversimplified version of leading ideas and attitudes of the age which preceded them — a myth of the Enlightenment (much as the Renaissance Humanists did regarding the Middle Ages). By making clear what they opposed, their oversimplification helped to identify themselves, their age, their very purposes. Modern historians and students of Romanticism have had to take into consideration this view the Romantics had of themselves, while remaining prepared to discount the distortion it introduced. In defining Romanticism they have nonetheless been forced to establish a contrast in order to discriminate between the old and the new intelligibly. Some contrasts, of course, can facilitate comprehension at the expense of awareness of the complexity of the history of ideas.

Textbook treatments too often gloss over the complexity of the interrelation of the ideas, and of the disagreements among the interpretations. They present the reader with a listing and exemplification of the series of novelties in art forms and aesthetics, in taste and sentiment, sometimes in philosophy, historical thought, political science, and law. They deal with Romanticism as something given, as a component in the late eighteenth and the nineteenth century. Statements about "it" are confident assertions. Too seldom do they explicitly recognize the three central problems treated in the following selections: the problem of *definition* of Romanticism; the problem of *evaluation* of its implications and consequences; and the problem of *explanation* of its appearance.

The readings which follow make evident how closely these three problems are interrelated. Some definitions will be found to imply explanation — such as the identification of Romanticism as a permanent trait or tendency of mankind. Others seem to incorporate evaluation, as in the case of interpretations identifying Romanticism as the source of abhorrent contemporary isms.

While some authors express little or no concern over problems of definition, others treat the issues at length. Some view Romanticism as a recurrent characteristic of literature, or the arts, or of the attitudes, beliefs, or psychology of the artist — an expression of basic human traits. To others it is a distinctly *historical* phenomenon, an occurrence with a specific location in time and place — yet there are many disagreements as to what to designate as the occurrence.

The variety of definitions may imply or necessitate a variety of chronological delineations. Where and when did it begin — in the Garden of Eden, the Middle Ages, with Rousseau, the German *Sturm und Drang,* the English Gothic Revival, the French Revolution or Restoration? And when did it end — with the appearance of literary realism? Or are we, as some authors suggest, still in a Romantic Age?

The disagreements over definition have not simply increased confusion. One of the functions of definition can be simplification and clarification by the abstraction of aspects or elements from complex phenomena. One of the most encouraging consequences of the controversy over Romanticism seems to have been the recurrent effort to identify those ideas or sentiments which became prevalent around the time of the French Revolution — those which seem most basic in the sense that all the period's variety of creation in art, politics, and other fields of activity may be seen, at least from present perspective, as logical outgrowths of, or as necessarily related to, some few basic idea clusters or categories which might provide the basis for a definition.

It will quickly become apparent to the reader how significantly each treatment of Romanticism is affected by the author's purposes and intentions. If it is treated as a causative or conditioning agent, the explanation of its appearance is less central than the evaluation of its consequences. Conversely, if the author's object is primarily to comprehend its appearance, then chief attention will be given to its genesis and the explanation thereof. In either instance, the usefulness of the definition employed is conditioned by the purposes to which it is put.

Evaluations of Romanticism, which of course have conditioned the whole enterprise of definition and explanation, have been remarkable for their intensity. Much energy has been devoted to analysis of Romanticism as the source of twentieth-century problems. Romanticism has provided a fertile field for those who find it useful to single out some one or some group to blame for present discontents. Rousseau, who is still castigated for originating twentieth century totalitarianism, was one of the earliest "villains," and later there was widespread concern at the time of the Second World War over Romanticism as the ideological basis of Nazism. The controversy over the Germanness of Romanticism and the Romanticism of Nazism was particularly vehement. Echoes of it appear in some of the selections offered here.

Explanations of Romanticism have proposed that its origin was in man's fundamental distaste for discipline, or alternatively in man's power of creation and his urge to control his world. Other explanations attribute it to the failure or inadequacy of old cosmologies — producing a psychological need for new beliefs and assurances, or an artistic need for new art forms, techniques, or symbols. Social and economic explanations have been offered to account for the origin as well as the diversity in character and chronology of several forms of *Romanticism* — in each of the foregoing instances usually somewhat differently defined.

I have categorized the selections which follow on the basis of whether they seem most to emphasize definition or evaluation on the one hand, or explanation on the other. Though the distinctions remain somewhat arbitrary, I believe the points of disagreement among the authors emerge most clearly when presented in this order.

I have placed first the selection from J. J. Saunders because it gives a brief summary of most of the phenomena which will be referred to in later selections as comprehended in the several definitions of Romanticism. And despite the fact that Saunders sees little problem in defining Romanticism, he is decidedly concerned to evaluate it. His evaluation strongly resembles that of Irving Babbitt, a selection from whose difficult and contentious book, *Rousseau and Romanticism,* follows next. The historical portions included here do not allow for full expression of Babbitt's criticism of early twentieth century culture — yet it remains clear that his distaste for Romanticism grows from his association of it with characteristics of his own age he disliked. Babbitt felt that definition should depend upon past usage; the confusions of past usage lead Jacques Barzun in the next selection to seek to clarify matters by introducing a distinction between *intrinsic* and *historic* Romanticism, in a study wherein he directly opposes the evaluations offered by Saunders and Babbittt. He praises the Romanticists of the Romantic era for their creativity which he believes merits appreciative and sympathetic *historical* understanding. Just as in Babbitt's case, his association of Romanticism with basic traits of human nature bears some of the burden of explanation of its predominance around the time of the French Revolution, and just as did Babbitt's, his book proved to be addressed to issues, primarily political, which Barzun confronted in the forties.

The selection from Howard E. Hugo, which follows Barzun's, is less concerned with the problems of definition and evaluation than are those which precede. It does however suggest most strikingly the difficulty of truly comprehensive definition. He distinguishes a set of categories to allow for placement of ideas, works, and authors in relation to one another, and to illuminate the variety of their interrelationships. Arthur O. Lovejoy, whose work is next represented by two selections, raised most explicitly the problem of definition in his essay "On the Discrimination of Romanticisms." In this we see his opposition to single, comprehensive definitions as well as his suggestions for meeting the problems of definition, and some exemplification of these suggestions in practice. The idea clusters basic to Romanticism which Lovejoy proposes, and which prove to be predominantly philosophic views, should be compared with the rather different categories Hugo offers. It is notable, too, that even so philosophic a scholar as Lovejoy felt moved to include in his *The Great Chain of Being* the balanced evaluation of Romanticism in reference to twentieth century isms with which we conclude the second selection from his works. Note how carefully Lovejoy avoids the sorts of comprehensive definitions shown in the earlier selections. For him Romanticism is simply a name to be given to common characteristics of evidence — quite unlike the reified concept we so commonly meet, where it occasionally appears that Romanticism is an active agent in history.

The selection from René Wellek directly contradicts Lovejoy's contentions. It

seems evident to Wellek that there do exist real similarities in those things traditionally designated as Romantic, and hence he argues that there was *one* Romantic movement rather than several quite different movements.

The concluding selections in Part I are from two Italians, Benedetto Croce and Mario Praz. Croce's is the more evaluative. He distinguishes, without much discussion, theoretical and moral Romanticism, praising the former and castigating the latter. He shows no hesitation over the unity of the movement, agreeing in this with Wellek, nor is he troubled over definition once his distinction is established. Praz, on the contrary, is more concerned over definition; aware of the difficulties involved, he nonetheless advocates the continued usage of Romanticism as an historical category.

As has already been suggested, nearly all the selections in Part I are to some degree concerned with explanation of the Romanticism therein defined or evaluated. Barzun is perhaps most explicit, emphasizing as he does the role of the French Revolution which destroyed the old, thus allowing for the predominance of Romantic creativity. The last two selections in Part I openly disagree over the explanation of Romanticism. Croce suggested that Romanticism arose from a lack of faith. Praz directly opposes this "metaphysical explanation" and finds the cause of Romanticism in tastes created by art works.

Croce's view may be taken as representative of attempts, chiefly by philosophers, to find an explanation for Romanticism in the problems posed by the inadequacy of old cosmologies. In the first selection in Part II the literary critic, R. A. Foakes, accepts this view but is most concerned that such inadequacy created a need for new artistic symbols. Others have sought to provide an intelligible rationale for the appearance of Romanticism in the *social* changes contemporaneously occurring; these are exemplified by Arnold Hauser and Edwin Berry Burgum. By a social and economic explanation Hauser and Burgum seek to account not merely for the appearance but for the diversity in character and chronology of Romanticism. Concluding the second part of this pamphlet are selections from three more specialized examinations of the relations of Romanticism to its milieu, here in three national contexts; the essay by G. S. R. Kitson Clark serves to remind us of the problems associated with generalizing about the relevance to politics or industrial change of a change in taste or ideas such as Romanticism; the selection from A. J. George singles out for assessment the specific relationships of Romanticism to the French industrial revolution; and that from Eugene Anderson sees German Romanticism as the result of psychological needs stemming primarily from a revolutionary social situation.

It is the purpose of this pamphlet to exemplify and to illuminate the controversy over Romanticism as it has developed since the 1920's. It would be impossible to represent the whole history of the study of Romanticism, which has produced a rich literature in nearly every major European language; and an effort to trace it through the major documents and significant studies which have appeared since 1800 would necessitate a volume or volumes of much larger compass. It has seemed most useful to introduce the student to recent analyses, several of which offer some retrospect over the work of the preceding century. I have also found it preferable to restrict the bulk of the selections to discussions of Romanticism in literature, philosophy, and politics, leaving aside any extended analyses of music or painting. The specialist's knowledge of the history of music and painting and the specialized language of criticism therein employed would require too much space for a brief pamphlet such as this. And for the student of history, it is perhaps easier to move from the analyses of Romanticism to the great written documents of its history which are so easily available, than it is to undertake the study of the great music and paintings of the Romantic era. It is to be hoped, of course, that the serious student will wish to pursue his study into these areas.

There remains, I trust, sufficient variety in the selections offered to suggest the range of controversial issues that scholars have treated. While these should lead the student to the documents, the selections themselves may be studied not only as important treatments of the subject, but also as themselves historical documents, partly explicable in the light of their authors' historical and personal concerns. The chief intention, however, has been to make possible the student's beginning to develop ways of describing and interpreting Romanticism which may be useful in his further study of history, and perhaps also of philosophy, political theory, and the arts.

[NOTE: The footnotes included in many of the original publications from which these readings have been taken are not reprinted in this book.]

The Conflict of Opinion

I — THE MEANINGS AND EVALUATION OF ROMANTICISM

"The word 'romantic' has come to mean so many things that, by itself, it means nothing. It has ceased to perform the function of a verbal sign. The new ideas of the period . . . were in large part heterogeneous, logically independent, and sometimes essentially antithetic to one another in their implications."

— ARTHUR O. LOVEJOY

"If we examine the characteristics of the actual literature which called itself or was called 'romantic' all over the continent, we find throughout Europe the same conceptions of poetry and of the workings and nature of poetic imagination, the same conception of nature and its relation to man, and basically the same poetic style, with a use of imagery, symbolism, and myth which is clearly distinct from that of eighteenth-century neo-classicism."

— RENÉ WELLEK

"Clearly, the one thing that unifies men in a given age is not their individual philosophies but the dominant problem that these philosophies are designed to solve. In the romantic period . . . this problem was to create a new world on the ruins of the old. . . . The results were to mark an epoch not only in art and society, but in political forms and natural science . . . it was a Biological Revolution."

— JACQUES BARZUN

"So Romanticism was absorbed into the Medieval tradition and continued to flourish until it was eclipsed by the classical revival inaugurated by the Renaissance. When it reemerged, at the close of the 18th century, its character had changed. It was restored only to artificial life, it had no roots in the culture of the new age, the dead forms of the past could never be properly resuscitated, it was forced to draw what vitality it could from sources which were alien to the older tradition and within two generations it was dead."

— J. J. SAUNDERS

II — EXPLANATIONS OF ROMANTICISM

"The characteristic feature of the romantic movement was not that it stood for a revolutionary or an anti-revolutionary, a progressive or a reactionary ideology, but that it reached both positions by a fanciful, irrational and undialectic route. . . . Romanticism was the ideology of the new society and the expression of the world-view of a generation which no longer believed in absolute values, could no longer believe in any values without thinking of their relativity, their historical limitations. . . . For romanticism was essentially a middle-class movement. . . ."

— ARNOLD HAUSER

"The fact of living in a time of cultural crisis conditioned the thinking and acting of the young German Romanticists as no other experience did. It forced them to deal not merely with a single aspect of life but with the totality of man, society and the universe. The crisis involved all values; it affected not merely the parts of man's existence but the whole. While compelling each person to seek his own salvation as best he could, it also forced him to look for support from the group. In the decade or so beginning with the late 1790's Romanticism offered a way of deliverance for persons caught in a crisis.

— EUGENE N. ANDERSON

". . . to be properly understood, romanticism must be considered not only as something which affected some of the leading minds of the day, it must be considered as a popular movement, even a vulgar movement."

— G. S. R. KITSON CLARK

". . . it is possible to conclude that the Industrial Revolution opened the way for a mass literature, and that the very machines which fashioned that age split romanticism into two factions, one of which continued the poetic revolution that the first generation had begun. To the other it presented new possibilities for artistic expression."

— ALBERT JOSEPH GEORGE

THE MEANINGS AND EVALUATION
OF ROMANTICISM

A Short-Lived Revival

J. J. SAUNDERS

The following selection from the historian J. J. Saunders' book, *The Age of Revolution*, offers a summary description of many of the ideas and tendencies most often considered Romantic. Unlike the other authors represented, Saunders denies that difficult historiographical problems are involved in delimiting and evaluating Romanticism. His own negative evaluation resembles that which appears in the succeeding selection from Irving Babbitt's attack upon Romanticism in *Rousseau and Romanticism*.

THE controversy between Classicism and Romanticism occupies considerable space in all histories of literature, for the rivals contended for the mastery of the world of letters for many centuries. There is a danger in using such distinctive labels, and some writers have made themselves ridiculous by their clumsy attempts to force almost every great literary figure of the past into one or other category. Still, no one can deny that two contrasting movements can be observed in literature and that now one and now the other has gained the ascendancy. Romanticism first made its appearance in Provence in the 12th century under Arab influences from Moorish Spain. The Renaissance produced a classical reaction which may be said to have triumphed by the middle of the 17th century and to have submerged its rival entirely during the age of Dryden and Pope, of Racine and Boileau. Largely under the spell of Rousseau, the wheel again came full circle and the beginning of the 19th century witnessed the great Romantic Revival.

To define the two terms is not difficult. Classicism inherited the literary traditions of Greece and Rome; it stood as Walter Pater said, for order in beauty, and resembled the cold perfection of a Doric column. The 18th century, or perhaps it would be better to say the century after 1660, is generally taken as its golden age. France was its acknowledged home: the civilized world accepted the standards of Versailles, and the courtiers of Louis XIV spoke a language which for clarity and polish has rarely been equaled. The literature of that time possesses certain unmistakable characteristics, such as a hatred of mystery and enthusiasm, the repression of emotion and imagination, obedience to supposedly Aristotelian rules, the conscious imitation of Greek and Latin models, especially the odes of Pindar and Horace and the satires of Juvenal, and a passion for clearness and regularity. The dramatist was haunted by the fear of violating the sacred "unities," and the poet was bound by rules as stiff as the etiquette of the drawing room. It mat-

From *The Age of Revolution* by J. J. Saunders, 1949, pp. 56–66, 67–69, by permission of **The Hutchinson Publishing Group.**

1

tered not so much what was said as how it was said. Correct style was everything, form was exalted over matter. . . . Only the 18th century would have dared to "improve" Shakespeare, and to deplore, as Voltaire did, his "monstrous irregularities." Literature had become urbanized: it rarely stirred outside the salon, the theater or the coffee-house, and the man of letters spent his time hanging round the mansions of the great on the look-out for a noble patron in return for whose favors he celebrated the pleasures of the town in faultless couplets. Poetry became a vehicle for little else but wit and satire directed not against sin but against dullness and unconventionality: the lyric was no longer cultivated, and in England at least the sonnet practically disappeared between Milton and Wordsworth. A sense of natural beauty was completely absent: the traveler abroad went to see the towns and hurried across the countryside as quickly as possible. . . .

Romanticism arose in the Middle Ages but it did not spring from Christian or even from Teutonic sources: it entered Europe through Moslem Spain and developed rapidly in the strange, exotic, orientalized culture of Provence, which after flourishing for over a century, was finally ruined in the Albigensian crusade. The songs of the troubadours strike an entirely new chord in European literature, for they introduced into Western civilization the ideals of chivalry and courtliness and the cult of womanhood and frustrated love. . . . The Arab-Provençal view of life — its carefree paganism, its joyful abandon, its frank carnality and women-worship — conquered the West, though the Christian religion purged it of some of its grosser elements and transformed the troubadour who sang of his love beneath his mistress's window into the chivalrous knight who swore before the altar of the Madonna to consecrate his sword to the defense of women and the faith.

So Romanticism was absorbed into the medieval tradition and continued to flourish until it was eclipsed by the classical revival inaugurated by the Renaissance. When it re-emerged, at the close of the 18th century, its character had changed. It was restored only to artificial life, it had no roots in the culture of the new age, the dead forms of the past could never be properly resuscitated, it was forced to draw what vitality it could from sources which were alien to the older tradition and within less than two generations it was dead. Yet this temporary revival, so productive in the field of art and letters, was not without its influence on the social, political and religious life of Europe. If the Romanticism of the 19th century was a somewhat spurious copy of the original, it at any rate drew attention to much that was of permanent value in the past and stressed an important aspect of reality which had long been overlooked.

The Romantic revival was a natural reply to a decadent classicism which had exhausted its vitality, and it therefore emphasized the points its predecessor had despised and ignored. It is often asserted that it was Rousseau who led the return to Nature and to the past. It is true that the tortured soul of Jean Jacques rebelled against the rules, conventions and artifices of a stilted and pompous society whose atmosphere choked and poisoned him. The solitary dreamer who paced the woods of Montmorency and exclaimed in ecstasy to be alone with Nature, far away from the world of men in which he felt himself a misfit, and who described in the "Nouvelle Héloise" how gladly he would have burst the barriers of convention which thwarted the gratification of his natural desires, was certainly the spiritual father of the revolt against the prosaic Age of Reason. But the revolutionary naturalism of Rousseau must be distinguished from the return to the Middle Ages. The one looked to the future, the other harked back to the past. There are points of contact but not complete identity. Rousseau brought people out of the drawing room and showed them the beauty of lake and mountain, but he was not the precursor of Scott and Victor Hugo.

The essential contrast between the aims

and ideas of the Romantics and those of the men of the 18th century could not be better put than in the words of the French historian Weill: "The epoch of Voltaire loved clear and precise prose; the Romantics preferred verse or poetic prose. The 18th century glorified reason and logic; they gave predominance to intuition and passion. The *philosophes* were absorbed by the social man, with the desire of bettering society; the Romantics celebrated the isolated individual, the sad and noble soul, who rebels against social rules and the oppression of the inept and mediocre crowd. The Encyclopedists had only disdain for the past; firmly persuaded that humanity obeys the laws of progress, they were interested in the present and thought to prepare well for a better future. The Romantics, shocked by the vulgarities of the present, sought refuge in the past which they idealized. The Voltairians fought the Church and at most preserved a natural religion, above all simplified and desiccated; the Romantics, penetrated by a religious spirit, had a marked sympathy for Catholicism because the art and poetry of countless generations had embellished it. Finally, in the strict domain of literature, the Romantics declared useless and obsolete the methods and rules of classical literature; they opposed the drama to the tragedy, substituted for the noble genre a richer and more varied style and completely remodelled versification."

Rousseau contributed to the Romantic movement its imaginative sensibility, its cult of wild nature, of the strange, the exotic, and the grotesque, its passionate individualism and craving for freedom, and its often morbid introspection. Medievalism, the new forms of lyric poetry, and the historical novel and drama, were later elements which developed first in England and Germany, were introduced into France by Madame de Staël and others, and were absorbed into the already dominant naturalism and sensibility. Romanticism as a fully developed philosophy of art and life made a stronger appeal to the Teutonic nations than to the Latin. The classicists maintained an obstinate resistance to it in France, and it never acquired a firm hold on Spain or Italy. Nonetheless, it penetrated fairly deeply into European culture, occupying, as it were, the void left by the decay of the old positive religious tradition. Its gravest weaknesses — its irrational emotionalism, its unhealthy morbidity, its glorification of instinct and its failure to work out a new scale of values to replace the abandoned ideals of the past — are to be traced to Rousseau, its saner and healthier elements are those which were contributed by others.

Germany and England led the way: the *Lyrical Ballads* of Wordsworth and Coleridge appeared in 1798, the same year in which Tieck and the Schlegel brothers launched the *Athenæum* in Berlin. Their common aim was to emancipate poetry from the tyranny of classicism by the invention of new literary forms or the revival of old ones in which the new sense of beauty and especially the appreciation of natural scenery could be best expressed. The English Romantics found in Nature, wild and untamed, the inspiration they were seeking, and they experimented with the lyric, the sonnet, blank verse, the stanza, the ballad and other forms into which to pour a poetic fervor which the old heroic couplet could no longer sustain. They turned men's attention from the cities, the artificial creation of human hands, to the countryside, where the handiwork of the Creator luxuriated in its natural loveliness. Burns taught his readers the attractions of the broad Scottish lowlands; the Lake poets worshipped Nature with such an intensity that they insensibly slipped into a pantheism which saw God in every created thing, the all-pervading spirit of the universe. Wordsworth conveys to us the loneliness and stark grandeur of the mountain, Shelley the furious energy of the wind, Keats the delightsome awe of dusky woods and mossy banks. The child and the peasant are extolled; their simplicity and contact with Nature exempt them from the vices of civilization. The traveler is exhorted to recognize the sublimity of hill and valley, of lake and waterfall, and to see in the rustic cottage, a ruined abbey, a field-mouse or the daffodils by the river-bank an intrinsic beauty which might for a moment link one to the Infinite. The classicists had never bothered about such things: to them they were trivial, vulgar, and unworthy of serious attention. The Romantics opened up a new world of pleasure and delight: their lyric song charmed a generation which had been shut up in salons and coffee-houses. It was perhaps fortunate that an appreciation of natural beauty should have been aroused among the peoples of the West just before the quiet and peaceful countryside was given over to the voracious grasp of industrialism and blackened and ruined by the smoke of furnaces. Paradoxical as it may seem, the same generation that claimed to have rediscovered the beauties of nature built the hideous slums and factories of the modern industrial towns.

The return to nature and the re-creation of lyrical poetry marked the first breach with the classical tradition. The second was the revival of the romantic novel, in a form considerably different, however, from the stilted and long-winded pastoral tales of early 17th century France. Beginning in England as a sort of "ghost-thriller" with Horace Walpole's *Castle of Otranto* (1764) and the "Gothic" stories of Mrs. Radcliffe and "Monk" Lewis, with their haunted castles, earthy vaults, specters and demons, and torturing inquisitors, it gradually developed into the historical novel of which Sir Walter Scott (1771–1832) became the acknowledged master. The "mystery" element was relegated to the background, and the novelist concentrated on reproducing the atmosphere of the past with as close a fidelity to historical fact as circumstances permitted. The scene of Scott's early books was laid in 18th century Scotland, which he knew best; then he went back to the Middle Ages and the 16th and 17th centuries, and shifted the scene to England or even to the Continent, as in *Quentin Dur-*

ward. The novel received entirely new treatment at his hands. Florid and fantastic romances there had been in abundance; psychological studies of character were well known, and the novel of manners, which attained almost perfection with Scott's contemporary, Jane Austen, had been brilliantly developed during the 18th century, but to take an historical event — the Porteous riots, the Crusade of Cœur-de-Lion, Louis XI's struggle with Charles the Bold — and to weave round it a tale which was given an increased illusion of reality by reason of its historical setting and its wonderfully descriptive "local color" was a new and highly successful departure. Scott's works won an enormous popularity throughout Europe, and especially in France, where De Vigny's *Cinq Mars* (1826), Merimée's *Chronique du règne de Charles IX* (1829) and Victor Hugo's *Notre-Dame de Paris* (1831), to say nothing of the rollicking, swashbuckling tales of Alexandre Dumas, clearly proclaim their debt to the Wizard of the North.

German Romanticism followed the path traced out for it by Herder under whose inspiration poets and dramatists shook themselves free from dependence on foreign models and began to draw upon the inexhaustible riches of the popular literature of the Teutonic past — the Volkslieder, the Northern epics, medieval legends, local folklore, myths and fairy tales. The lachrymose novel of sensibility was not absent: Goethe's *Wilhelm Meister* provoked a host of imitations, the most successful being the sentimental romances of Jean Paul Richter (1763–1825), whose deep spirituality and vivid sense of the unseen appealed not only to his own countrymen but also to English critics like Carlyle and De Quincey. But sensibility is only one aspect of Romanticism. The return to the past was heralded by Tieck (1773–1853), whose poems, dramas, novels and short stories reveal the influence of medieval literature and whose play *Kaiser Oktavianus* (1804) is a long glorification of the Middle Ages in which knights and shepherds, pilgrims and wanderers, princes and peasants, move across the stage. The Schlegels delved into the literature of all nations in their quest for romantic elements and new forms and scenes: August translated Shakespeare into German with such fidelity as almost to make him a national poet, while his brother Friedrich may almost be regarded as the founder of modern philology by the treatise he published in 1808 on the Sanskrit language. Between them they put German literary criticism on a sound basis; they aimed to reconcile the critic and the criticized, and laid it down that the former's duty is not to censure but to understand and to interpret. August's lectures on dramatic art and literature, which he delivered at Vienna in 1809–11, directly instigated Madame de Staël to compose her famous book *De l'Allemagne* (1813), which introduced German culture to her countrymen and launched the Romantic movement in France. Meanwhile the "Heidelberg school," of which Brentano and Von Arnim were the leading members, were busy collecting the old German folk songs with an assiduity only equaled by Scott's care in preserving the Border lays and ballads, and the brothers Grimm varied their philological studies by writing the charming fairy tales in which the spirit of the old "märchen" is admirably preserved. Though the great Goethe held aloof and maintained a standpoint of sane and level humanism, Romanticism received a tremendous impetus after the patriotic hysteria of 1813, when the stirring martial songs its leaders composed were chanted all over Germany.

Even contemporary philosophy received a Romantic impress. The individualism of Kant, who held that the lowest human consciousness constitutes what is real and that the most degraded man can thus attain to true "freedom," was developed by Fichte, whose philosophy is based on the Ego, of which the moral world is the conscious creation. He preached self-denial and renunciation with the fervor of a medieval ascetic, and insisted that every man must carve out his own destiny — an unbridled individualism that was partially responsible for the excesses into which so many of the Romantics fell. Following Fichte a comprehensive theory of aesthetic was formulated by Schelling (1775–1854), who regarded Nature and Spirit as two aspects of the "world soul" (Weltseele). "Nature is Spirit visible, Spirit is Nature invisible." The two are blended in art, which reveals to us not only the thing as it is, but enables us to understand the Spirit of which the natural object is but the outward form. Art thus appears superior both to nature and to philosophy, and "art for art's sake" soon became the watchword of the Romantics.

French Romanticism was an importation from Germany and England and proved a short-lived phenomenon. According to Sainte-Beuve, Rousseau was its grandfather and Chateaubriand its father. The author of *Atala* and *Réné* undoubtedly restored a sense of artistic composition to French literature: the cold and hard glitter, which a dry, unimaginative and somewhat shallow rationalism had imparted to it had grown wearisome and unsatisfying. Chateaubriand's warm and sensitive prose, rising at times to an almost poetic eloquence, was never so effective as when describing Red Indian life in the forests of North America before the white man had penetrated the "backwoods" and had slaughtered or driven away its primitive inhabitants, and his description of Niagara Falls by moonlight is a perfect gem of its kind. Unlike Rousseau, Chateaubriand is more interested in scenery for its own sake than for the emotions which it excites. A fully-fledged Romanticism did not appear until Madame de Staël's account of Germany and the new literary movement in vogue there was published in 1813, and Scott's novels and Byron's poems began to attract attention in France. Lamartine's *Meditations* (1820), which the dry and unemotional Talleyrand sat up half the night reading, proclaimed the conversion of France's younger generation of writers. Throughout the 1820's, Hugo, De Vigny,

Merimée, Sainte-Beuve and other youthful rebels against the classical tradition fought a furious battle against the strongly-entrenched Academy and all it stood for, the struggle being strangely allied to the Liberal political attack on the Bourbon régime. Hugo indeed defined Romanticism as "liberalism in literature," for was it not part of the universal fight for freedom and self-expression against decadent and tyrannical orthodoxies? Historical novels à la Scott, lyrical poetry, and romantic drama were all taken up with passionate enthusiasm. When an English company played Shakespeare in Paris in 1827, Dumas declared in ecstasy, "Only then did I realize what drama could be — this was the first time I had seen real passions on the stage," and immediately he set to work writing *Henri III et sa Cour,* which the young bloods cheered to the echo when it was acted in 1829. Hugo in the preface to *Cromwell* (1828), delivered a violent attack on the whole classic theater of Corneille and Racine, and asserted that tragedy, far from being a restrained work of art, should depict real life naturally and that the comic and grotesque element must not be excluded. To the classicist the grave-diggers' scene in *Hamlet* was intolerable and disgusting in the extreme; to the Romantic it brought one face to face with reality and was an essential part of the drama.

The Revolution of 1830 was hailed by Hugo and his circle as a Romantic triumph. In theater, in café, in newspaper they had branded kings and nobles as enemies of the human race, and hailed the dawn of liberty. The hysterical ardor which was willing to push France into a war with half Europe for the liberation of the struggling Poles and Italians, had its counterpart in England in the revolutionary fury of Shelley, whose esoteric drama *Prometheus Unbound,* depicts the human race bursting the shackles of conventions and traditional orthodoxies, the mysticism of Blake and his dreams of the new Jerusalem "in England's green and pleasant land," and the quixotic sacrifice of Byron, who ended his Childe Harold's pilgrimage at Missolonghi (1824), dying in the cause of Greek independence. The Romantics' dissatisfaction with the present produced not only an idealization of the past but the fervent hope of remodeling the world in the future.

The revolution in literature left its mark on nearly all departments of culture. The awakening of interest in the past led naturally to a closer investigation into the antiquities of nations and peoples. The historical novelist was quickly followed by the romantic historian, and a public stimulated by the novels of Scott and Bulwer Lytton, of Hugo and Dumas, turned for confirmation of the picturesque and remote life therein described to the vivid and absorbing narratives of Thierry and Michelet, of Carlyle and Lamartine. . . . Even among the less advanced Slavonic nations there was a kind of cultural renaissance; their scholars brought to light half-forgotten myths, tales and legends of their heroic age, and so helped to kindle in them an ardent longing to emulate the glorious deeds of their primitive ancestors. Romanticism was not a little responsible for the nationalist outbreaks of 1848.

Romanticism even invaded the domain of law. In Germany Savigny (1779–1861) severely criticized the theory of Natural Law as embodied in the Declaration of the Rights of Man and the Napoleonic Code which the revolutionary conquerors had imposed upon all countries subjugated by their arms. Man as an isolated individual is a fiction, according to Savigny, for it is impossible to divorce him from his tribe, family, class or nation. Natural law does not exist. Only to historic law rooted in a people's past, and changed, modified and adapted to suit particular conditions, can reality be applied. If such were the cause, it were folly to ignore local customs and usages, however irrational they might appear, for they were probably founded on the peculiar necessity of the place and time had proved their utility and value. The influence of Herder is clearly traceable here. The defenders of Natural Law attacked

Savigny and his school as die-hard traditionalists, and upholders of ancient prejudices and out-worn superstitions, but they found little support in Germany after the anti-French reaction that followed the War of Liberation.

In the field of art the Romantics triumphed after a long struggle. Rejecting the classical theory of absolute beauty, the same in all ages and places, they held that esthetic standards varied according to circumstances, and that the imitation of antique models, the expressions of a long dead culture, was no true art. Instead of exquisite nudes modeled on classical sculpture and used to illustrate scenes of ancient mythology, the Romantics, following the example of the 17th century Dutch artists, sought to portray the simple and humble scenes of real life and the beauties of land and seascape. The human figure ceased to occupy the center of the canvas, and the dethronement of man was succeeded by the elevation of wild nature as the chief subject of the painter's inspiration. In place of Venuses and Dianas, of lords and ladies, the salons exhibited pictures of forest and river bank; of ships at sea and peasants in the field. The landscapes of Turner and Constable in England, of Delacroix and the Barbizon school, led by Corot and Millet, in France, were significant of the "dehumanizing" tendencies of the "return to nature" school. Medievalism in art was represented by the Pre-Raphælites, who, attracted by the freshness and simplicity of the Christian art of the later Middle Ages, went back behind the Renaissance and modeled their work on the frescoes of Cimabue, Giotto and Fra Angelico. . . . Architecture followed the same path; neo-Gothic churches and public buildings sprang up which contrasted strangely with stark ugliness of the new factories of industrialism.

Romanticism was destined to a short life. It was vitiated by grave defects and many of its leaders discredited the movement by the excesses into which they plunged. Like Rousseau, it was self-conscious, neurotic and unbalanced. The restraint, the decorum, the order which had characterized classicism was thrown to the winds, and the freedom of the Romantics speedily degenerated into licence, a quest for mere novelty, an outrageous flouting of accepted conventions, a determination to be different from other men, combined with a spiritual and ethical indolence which precluded them from erecting new standards of life and conduct. Their eccentricities grew intolerable. The men of the old régime sought to conform to a set pattern, and utterly disdained the unusual and the grotesque; the Romantic glories in his uniqueness. The first page of the *Confessions* proclaims Rousseau's conviction that he stands alone in the annals of humanity, and both he and his successors sought to advertise their individuality by every extravagance that suggested itself. The Armenian costume of Jean-Jacques, "the diabolical glint and corpse-like complexion" of Byron and the flamboyant youth of 1830, and the blue china and green carnations of Oscar Wilde, are trivial externalities which nonetheless throw much light on the Romantic mentality. The acute sensibility and morbidly quivering introspection, illustrated by Rousseau's tears, Wordsworth's dejection of melancholy, Shelley's almost feminine lamentations, and the general nostalgia which afflicts the poets of this age, drew forth Goethe's contemptuous remark that the Romantics wrote "as though they were ill, and as though the whole world were a hospital." Their failure to establish a satisfactory criterion of moral values in place of the old Christian tradition left them with no secure anchor in life. After having proclaimed with Rousseau, that man is naturally good and sin therefore an illusion, and having shifted the burden of guilt from the individual to society and reduced the moral conscience to a mere sentiment, happiness still eluded the rebels. Actions counted for less than feelings. "Her conduct was reprehensible but her heart was pure," says Rousseau, describing the strange amours of Madame de Warens, and the

Romantics drifted helplessly along the current of emotion, only too often perishing among the rocks and shoals. Romanticism, disillusioned and dispirited, gave way before the middle of the century to the hard and bitter Realism which was to culminate in the horrible neurasthenia of the "fin de siècle."

The Qualities of Rousseauism

IRVING BABBITT

Irving Babbitt (1865–1933) was for most of his career professor of French literature at Harvard University. His chief contribution to scholarship in that field was his *Masters of Modern French Criticism* (1912). His greatest interest, however, was in comparative literature, an interest exemplied by his *Rousseau and Romanticism*, from which the following selection is drawn. *Rousseau and Romanticism* was also representative of Babbitt's ties to the "New Humanism" proclaimed also by Paul Elmer Moore and others, which sought to apply classical humanistic standards to all departments of life, in opposition to modern movements in literature and criticism.

THE words classic and romantic, we are often told, cannot be defined at all, and even if they could be defined, some would add, we should not be much profited. But this inability or unwillingness to define may itself turn out to be only one aspect of a movement that from Rousseau to Bergson has sought to discredit the analytical intellect — what Wordsworth calls "the false secondary power by which we multiply distinctions." However, those who are with Socrates rather than with Rousseau or Wordsworth in this matter, will insist on the importance of definition, especially in a chaotic era like the present; for nothing is more characteristic of such an era than its irresponsible use of general terms. Now to measure up to the Socratic standard, a definition must not be abstract and metaphysical, but experimental; it must not, that is, reflect our opinion of what a word should mean, but what it actually has meant. Mathematicians may be free at times to frame their own definitions, but in the case of words like classic and romantic, that have been used innumerable times, and used not in one but in many countries, such a method is inadmissible. One must keep one's eye on actual usage. . . .

Now to define in a Socratic way two things are necessary: one must learn to see a common element in things that are apparently different and also to discriminate between things that are apparently similar. A Newton, to take the familiar instance of the former process, saw a common element in the fall of an apple and the motion of a planet; and one may perhaps without being a literary Newton discover a common element in all the main uses of the word romantic as well as in all the main uses of the word classic; though some of the things to which the word romantic in particular has been applied seem, it must be admitted, at least as far apart as the fall of an apple and the motion of a planet. The first step is to perceive the something that connects two or more of these things apparently so diverse, and then it may be found necessary to refer this unifying trait itself back to something still more general, and so on until we arrive, not indeed at anything absolute — the absolute will always elude us — but at what Goethe calls the original or underlying phenomenon (*Urphänomen*). A fruitful source of false definition is to take as primary in a more or less closely allied group of facts what is actually secondary — for example, to fix upon the return to the

From *Rousseau and Romanticism* by Irving Babbitt (Boston, 1919), selections from pp. 1–366. By permission of Houghton Mifflin Company.

Middle Ages as the central fact in romanticism, whereas this return is only symptomatic; it is very far from being the original phenomenon. Confused and incomplete definitions of romanticism have indeed just that origin — they seek to put at the centre something that though romantic is not central but peripheral, and so the whole subject is thrown out of perspective.

My plan then is to determine to the best of my ability, . . . the common element in the various uses of the words classic and romantic; and then, having thus disposed of the similarities, to turn to the second part of the art of defining and deal, also historically, with the differences. For my subject is not romanticism in general, but only a particular type of romanticism, and this type of romanticism needs to be seen as a recoil, not from classicism in general, but from a particular type of classicism. . . .

In general a thing is romantic when, as Aristotle would say, it is wonderful rather than probable; in other words, when it violates the normal sequence of cause and effect in favor of adventure. Here is the fundamental contrast between the words classic and romantic which meets us at the outset and in some form or other persists in all the uses of the word down to the present day. A thing is romantic when it is strange, unexpected, intense, superlative, extreme, unique, etc. A thing is classical, on the other hand, when it is not unique, but representative of a class. In this sense medical men may speak correctly of a classic case of typhoid fever, or a classic case of hysteria. One is even justified in speaking of a classic example of romanticism. By an easy extension of meaning a thing is classical when it belongs to a high class or to the best class. . . .

. . . Like all the great Greeks Aristotle recognizes that man is the creature of two laws: he has an ordinary or natural self of impulse and desire and a human self that is known practically as a power of control over impulse and desire. If man is to become human he must not let impulse and desire run wild, but must oppose to everything excessive in his ordinary self, whether in thought or deed or emotion, the law of measure. This insistence on restraint and proportion is rightly taken to be of the essence not merely of the Greek spirit but of the classical spirit in general. . . .

After this attempt to define briefly with the help of the Greeks the classical spirit in its essence we should be prepared to understand more clearly the way in which this spirit was modified in neo-classical times, especially in France. The first thing that strikes one about the classicism of this period is that it does not rest on immediate perception like that of the Greeks but on outer authority. The merely dogmatic and traditional classicist gave a somewhat un-Greek meaning to the doctrines of nature and imitation. Why imitate nature directly, said Scaliger, when we have in Virgil a second nature? Imitation thus came to mean the imitation of certain outer models and the following of rules based on these models. . . .

. . . When men became conscious in the eighteenth century of the neo-classical meagerness on the imaginative side they began to look back with a certain envy to the free efflorescence of fiction in the Middle Ages. They began to ask themselves with Hurd whether the reason and correctness they had won were worth the sacrifice of a "world of fine fabling." . . . The type of romanticism, however, which came in towards the end of the eighteenth century did not, even when professedly mediæval, simply revert to the older types. It was primarily not a romanticism of thought or of action, . . . but a romanticism of feeling. The beginnings of this emotional romanticism antedate considerably the application of the word romantic to a particular literary school. Before considering how the word came to be thus applied we shall need to take a glance at eighteenth-century sentimentalism, especially at the plea for genius and originality that, from about the middle of the century on, were opposed to the tameness and servile imitation of the neo-classicists. . . .

. . . What the genius wanted was spontaneity, and spontaneity, as he understood it, involves a denial, not merely of decorum, but of something that, . . . goes deeper than decorum — namely the doctrine of imitation. According to Voltaire genius is only judicious imitation. According to Rousseau the prime mark of genius is refusal to imitate. . . .

. . . To follow nature in the classical sense is to imitate what is normal and representative in man and so to become decorous. To be natural in the new sense one must begin by getting rid of imitation and decorum. Moreover, for the classicist, nature and reason are synonymous. The primitivist, on the other hand, means by nature the spontaneous play of impulse and temperament, and inasmuch as this liberty is hindered rather than helped by reason, he inclines to look on reason, not as the equivalent but as the opposite of nature. . . . The movement that took its rise in the eighteenth century involves, we should recollect, a break not with one but with two traditions — the classical and the Christian. If the plea for genius and originality is to be largely explained as a protest against the mechanical imitation and artificial decorum of a certain type of classicist, the assertion of man's natural goodness is to be understood rather as a rebound from the doctrine of total depravity that was held by the more austere type of Christian. . . . God, instead of being opposed to nature, is conceived by the deist as a power that expresses his goodness and loveliness through nature. The oppressive weight of fear that the older theology had laid upon the human spirit is thus gradually lifted. Man begins to discover harmonies instead of discords in himself and outer nature. He not only sees virtue in instinct but inclines to turn virtue itself into a "sense," or instinct. And this means in practice to put emotional expansion in

the place of spiritual concentration at the basis of life and morals. . . .

. . . This throwing off of the yoke of both Christian and classical discipline in the name of temperament is the essential aspect of the movement in favor of original genius. The genius does not look to any pattern that is set above his ordinary spontaneous ego and imitate it. On the contrary, he attains to the self-expression that other men, intimidated by convention, weakly forego. . . .

. . . Everything that limits temperamental expansion is dismissed as either artificial or mechanical; everything on the contrary that makes for the emancipation of temperament, and so for variety and difference, he welcomes as vital, dynamic, creative. . . .

. . . The conscious analysis that is needed if one is to establish orderly sequences and relationships and so work out a kingdom of ends is repudiated by the Rousseauist because it diminishes wonder, because it interferes with the creative impulse of genius as it gushes up spontaneously from the depths of the unconscious. The whole movement is filled with the praise of ignorance and of those who still enjoy its inappreciable advantages — the savage, the peasant and above all the child. The Rousseauist may indeed be said to have discovered the poetry of childhood of which only traces can be found in the past, but at what would seem at times a rather heavy sacrifice of rationality. Rather than consent to have the bloom taken off things by analysis one should, as Coleridge tells us, *sink back* to the devout state of childlike wonder. However, to grow ethically is not to sink back but to struggle painfully forward. To affirm the contrary is to set up the things that are below the ordinary rational level as a substitute for the things that are above it, and at the same time to proclaim one's inability to mature. The romanticist, it is true, is wont to oppose to the demand for maturity Christ's praise of the child. But Christ evidently praises the child not because of his capacity for wonder but because of his freedom from sin, and it is of the essence of Rousseauism to deny the very existence of sin — at least in the Christian sense of the word. One may also read in the New Testament that when one has ceased to be a child one should give up childish things, and this is a saying that no primitivist, so far as I am aware, has ever quoted. On the contrary, he is ready to assert that what comes to the child spontaneously is superior to the deliberate moral effort of the mature man. The speeches of all the sages are, according to Maeterlinck, outweighed by the unconscious wisdom of the passing child. Wordsworth hails a child of six as "Mighty Prophet! Seer blest!" (It is only fair to Coleridge to say that he refused to follow Wordsworth into this final abyss of absurdity.) In much the same way Hugo pushes his adoration of the child to the verge of what has been termed "solemn silliness" (*niaiserie solennelle*). . . .

. . . The general truth at which the classicist aims the Rousseauist dismisses as identical with the gray and the academic, and bends all his efforts to the rendering of the vivid and unique detail. . . . He is ready to employ not only the homely and familiar word that the pseudo-classicist had eschewed as "low," but words so local and technical as to be unintelligible to ordinary readers. Chateaubriand deals so specifically with the North American Indian and his environment that the result, according to Sainte-Beuve, is a sort of "tattooing" of his style. Hugo bestows a whole dictionary of architectural terms upon the reader in his "Notre Dame," and of nautical terms in his "Toilers of the Sea." In order to follow some of the passages in Balzac's "César Birotteau," one needs to be a lawyer or a professional accountant, and it has been said that in order to do justice to a certain description in Zola one would need to be a pork-butcher. In this movement towards a highly specialized vocabulary one should note a coöperation, as so often elsewhere, between the two wings of the naturalistic

movement — the scientific and the emotional. The Rousseauist is, like the scientist, a specialist — he specializes in his own sensations. He goes in quest of emotional thrills for their own sake, just as Napoleon's generals, according to Sainte-Beuve, waged war without any ulterior aim but for the sheer lust of conquest. The vivid images and picturesque details are therefore not sufficiently structural; each one tends to thrust itself forward without reference to the whole and to demand attention for its own sake. . . .

. . . Poe was fond of quoting a saying of Bacon's that "there is no excellent beauty that hath not some strangeness in the proportion." This saying became known in France through Baudelaire's rendering of Poe and was often ascribed to Poe himself. It was taken to mean that the stranger one became the nearer one was getting to perfect beauty. And if we grant this view of beauty we must admit that some of the decadents succeeded in becoming very beautiful indeed. But the more the element of proportion in beauty is sacrificed to strangeness the more the result will seem to the normal man to be, not beauty at all, but rather an esoteric cult of ugliness. The romantic genius therefore denounces the normal man as a philistine and at the same time, since he cannot please him, seeks at least to shock him and so capture his attention by the very violence of eccentricity. . . .

It is fair to say that in lieu of the discipline of culture the romantic genius has often insisted on the discipline of technique; and this has been especially true in a country like France with its persistent tradition of careful workmanship. Gautier, for example, would have one's "floating dream sealed" in the hardest and most resisting material, that can only be mastered by the perfect craftsman; and he himself, falling into a confusion of the arts, tries to display such a craftsmanship by painting and carving with words. Flaubert, again, refines upon the technique of writing to a point where it becomes not merely a discipline but a torture. But if a man is to be a romantic genius in the fullest sense he must, it should seem, repudiate even the discipline of technique as well as the discipline of culture in favor of an artless spontaneity. For after all the genius is only the man who retains the virtues of the child, and technical proficiency is scarcely to be numbered among these virtues. The German romanticists already prefer the early Italian painters because of their naïveté and divine awkwardness to the later artists who had a more conscious mastery of their material. The whole Pre-Raphaelite movement is therefore only one aspect of Rousseau's return to nature. To later primitivists the early Italians themselves seem far too deliberate. They would recover the spontaneity displayed in the markings on Alaskan totem poles or in the scratchings of the caveman on the flint. A prerequisite to pure genius, if we are to judge by their own productions, is an inability to draw. . . .

An eccentricity so extreme as to be almost or quite indistinguishable from madness is then the final outcome of the revolt of the original genius from the regularity of the eighteenth century. . . .

. . . This extreme romantic emancipation of the imagination was accompanied by an equally extreme emancipation of the emotions. Both kinds of emancipation are, as I have tried to show, a recoil partly from neo-classical judgment — a type of judgment which seemed to oppress all that is creative and spontaneous in man under a weight of outer convention; partly, from the reason of the Enlightenment, a type of reason that was so logical and abstract that it seemed to mechanize the human spirit, and to be a denial of all that is immediate and intuitive. . . .

. . . The retreat of the Rousseauist into some "land of chimeras" or tower of ivory assumes forms almost incredibly complex and subtle, but at bottom the ivory tower is only one form of man's ineradicable longing to escape from the oppression of the actual into some land of heart's desire, some golden age of fancy. . . .

Rousseau, then, owes his significance not only to the fact that he was supremely imaginative in an age that was disposed to deny the supremacy of the imagination, but to the fact that he was imaginative in a particular way. A great multitude since his time must be reckoned among his followers, not because they have held certain ideas but because they have exhibited a similar quality of imagination. In seeking to define this quality of imagination we are therefore at the very heart of our subject.

It is clear from what has already been said that Rousseau's imagination was in a general way Arcadian, and this, if not the highest, is perhaps the most prevalent type of imagination. . . .

. . . Moreover, the definitely primitivistic coloring that he gave to his imaginative renewal of the pastoral dream appealed to an age that was reaching the last stages of over-refinement. . . .

To the romantic conception of the ideal can be traced the increasing lack of understanding between the poet, or in general the creator, and the public during the past century. Many neoclassical writers may, like Boileau, have shown an undue reverence for what they conceived to be the general sense of their time, but to measure one's inspiration by one's remoteness from this general sense is surely a far more dangerous error; and yet one was encouraged to do this very thing by the views of original genius that were held in the eighteenth century. Certain late neo-classicists lacked imagination and were at the same time always harping on good sense. It was therefore assumed that to insist on good sense was necessarily proof of a lack of imagination. Because the attempt to achieve the universal had led to a stale and lifeless imitation it was assumed that a man's genius consists in his uniqueness, in his unlikeness to other men. Now nothing is more private and distinctive in a man than his feelings, so that to be unique meant practically for Rousseau and his followers to be unique in feeling. Feeling alone they held was vital and immediate. As a matter of fact the element in a man's nature that he possesses in common with other men is also something that he *senses,* something that is in short intuitive and immediate. But good sense the genius identifies with lifeless convention and so measures his originality by the distance of his emotional and imaginative recoil from it. Of this warfare between sense and sensibility that begins in the eighteenth century, the romantic war between the poet and the philistine is only the continuation. This war has been bad for both artist and public. If the artist has become more and more eccentric, it must be confessed that the good sense of the public against which he has protested has been too flatly utilitarian. . . .

The problem, then, of the genius or the artist versus the philistine has persisted without essential modification from the eighteenth century to the present day — from the suicide of Chatterton, let us say, to the suicide of John Davidson. The man of imagination spurns in the name of his "ideal" the limits imposed upon it by a dull respectability, and then his ideal turns out only too often to lack positive content and to amount in practice to the expansion of infinite indeterminate desire. What the idealist opposes to the real is not only something that does not exist, but something that never can exist. The Arcadian revery which should be allowed at most as an occasional solace from the serious business of living is set up as a substitute for living. The imaginative and emotional dalliance of the Rousseauistic romanticist may assume a bewildering variety of forms. . . . The momentous matter is not that a man's imagination and emotions go out towards this or that particular haven of refuge in the future or in the past, in the East or in the West, but that his primary demand on life is for some haven or refuge; that he longs to be away from the here and now and their positive demands on his character and will. Poe may sing of "the glory that was Greece and the grandeur that was Rome," but he is not therefore a classicist.

With the same wistfulness innumerable romanticists have looked towards the Middle Ages. . . .

Nostalgia, the term that has come to be applied to the infinite indeterminate longing of the romanticist — his never-ending quest after the ever-fleeting object of desire — is not, from the point of view of strict etymology, well-chosen. Romantic nostalgia is not "homesickness," accurately speaking, but desire to get away from home. Odysseus in Homer suffers from true nostalgia. The Ulysses of Tennyson, on the other hand, is nostalgic in the romantic sense when he leaves home "to sail beyond the sunset." . . . Music is exalted by the romanticists above all other arts because it is the most nostalgic, the art that is most suggestive of the hopeless gap between the "ideal" and the "real." . . . In musical and other nostalgia, the feelings receive a sort of infinitude from the coöperation of the imagination; and this infinitude, this quest of something that must ever elude one, is at the same time taken to be the measure of one's idealism. The symmetry and form that the classicist gains from working within bounds are no doubt excellent, but then the willingness to work within bounds betokens a lack of aspiration. If the primitivist is ready, as some one has complained, to turn his back on the bright forms of Olympus and return to the ancient gods of chaos and of night, the explanation is to be sought in this idea of the infinite. It finally becomes a sort of Moloch to which he is prepared to sacrifice most of the values of civilized life. The chief fear of the classicist is to be thought monstrous. The primitivist on the contrary is inclined to see a proof of superior amplitude of spirit in mere grotesqueness and disproportion. The creation of monsters is, as Hugo says, a "satisfaction due to the infinite."

The breaking down by the emotional romanticist of the barriers that separate not merely the different literary genres but the different arts is only another aspect of his readiness to follow the lure of the infinite. . . .

. . . Every imaginable extreme, the extreme of reaction as well as the extreme of radicalism, goes with romanticism; every genuine mediation between extremes is just as surely unromantic. . . . The delicate point to determine about Friedrich Schlegel and many other romanticists is why they finally came to place their land of heart's desire in the Middle Ages rather than in Greece. In treating this question one needs to take at least a glance at the modification that Herder (whose influence on German romanticism is very great) gave to the primitivism of Rousseau. Cultivate your genius, Rousseau said in substance, your ineffable difference from other men, and look back with longing to the ideal moment of this genius — the age of childhood, when your spontaneous self was not as yet cramped by conventions or "sicklied o'er by the pale cast of thought." Cultivate your national genius, Herder said in substance, and look back wistfully at the golden beginnings of your nationality when it was still naïve and "natural," when poetry instead of being concocted painfully by individuals was still the unconscious emanation of the folk. Herder indeed expands primitivism along these lines into a whole philosophy of history. The romantic notion of the origin of the epic springs out of this soil, a notion that is probably at least as remote from the facts as the neo-classical notion — and that is saying a great deal. Any German who followed Herder in the extension that he gave to Rousseau's views about genius and spontaneity could not only see the folk soul mirrored at least as naïvely in the "Nibelungenlied" as in the "Iliad," but by becoming a mediæval enthusiast he could have the superadded pleasure of indulging not merely personal but racial and national idiosyncrasy. Primitivistic mediævalism is therefore an important ingredient, especially in the case of Germany, in romantic nationalism — the type that has flourished beyond all measure during the past century. Again, though one might, like Hölderlin, cherish an infinite longing for the Greeks, the Greeks themselves, at least the Greeks

of Schiller, did not experience longing; but this fact came to be felt more and more by F. Schlegel and other romanticists as an inferiority, showing as it did that they were content with the finite. As for the neo-classicists who were supposed to be the followers of the Greeks, their case was even worse; they not only lacked aspiration and infinitude, but were sunk in artificiality, and had moreover become so analytical that they must perforce see things in "disconnection dead and spiritless." The men of the Middle Ages, on the other hand, as F. Schlegel saw them, were superior to the neo-classicists in being naïve; their spontaneity and unity of feeling had not yet suffered from artificiality, or been disintegrated by analysis. At the same time they were superior to the Greeks in having aspiration and the sense of the infinite. The very irregularity of their art testified to this infinitude. It is not uncommon in the romantic movement thus to assume that because one has very little form one must therefore have a great deal of "soul." F. Schlegel so extended his definition of the mediæval spirit as to make it include writers like Shakespeare and Cervantes, who seemed to him to be vital and free from formalism. The new nationalism was also made to turn to the profit of the Middle Ages. Each nation in shaking off the yoke of classical imitation and getting back to its mediæval past was recovering what was primitive in its own genius, was substituting what was indigenous for what was alien to it. . . .

The distinction between classic and romantic worked out by the Schlegels and spread abroad by Madame de Staël was, then, largely associated with a certain type of mediævalism. Nevertheless one cannot insist too strongly that the new school deserved to be called romantic, not because it was mediæval, but because it displayed a certain quality of imagination in its mediævalism. The longing for the Middle Ages is merely a very frequent form of nostalgia, and nostalgia I have defined as the pursuit of pure illusion. No doubt a man may be mediæval in his leanings and yet very free from nostalgia. He may, for example, prefer St. Thomas Aquinas to any modern philosopher on grounds that are the very reverse of romantic; and in the attitude of any particular person towards the Middle Ages, romantic and unromantic elements may be mingled in almost any conceivable proportion; and the same may be said of any past epoch that one prefers to the present. . . . But the mediævalist, in so far as he is romantic, does not turn to a mediæval reality from a real but distasteful present. Here as elsewhere his first requirement is not that his "vision" should be true, but that it should be rich and radiant; and the more "ideal" the vision becomes in this sense, the wider the gap that opens between poetry and life. . . .

The Rousseauist especially feels an inner kinship with Prometheus and other Titans. He is fascinated by every form of insurgency. Cain and Satan are both romantic heroes. To meet the full romantic requirement, however, the insurgent must also be tender-hearted. He must show an elemental energy in his explosion against the established order and at the same time a boundless sympathy for the victims of it. . . .

The Rousseauist is ever ready to discover beauty of soul in any one who is under the reprobation of society. The figure of the courtesan rehabilitated through love that has enjoyed such popularity during the past hundred years goes back to Rousseau himself. The underlying assumption of romantic morality is that the personal virtues, the virtues that imply self-control, count as naught compared with the fraternal spirit and the readiness to sacrifice one's self for others. . . .

This subordination of all the other values of life to sympathy is achieved only at the expense of the great humanistic virtue — decorum or a sense of proportion. . . .

. . . The romantic moralist tends to favor expansion on the ground that it is vital, creative, infinite, and to dismiss whatever seems to set bounds to expansion as something inert, mechanical, finite. In its onslaughts on the veto power whether within or without the breast of the individual it is plain that no age has ever approached the age of original genius in the midst of which we are still living. . . .

The faith in one's natural goodness is a constant encouragement to evade moral responsibility. To accept responsibility is to follow the line of maximum effort, whereas man's secret desire is to follow, if not the line of least, at all events the line of lesser resistance. The endless twisting and dodging and proneness to look for scapegoats that results is surely the least reputable aspect of human nature. Rousseau writes to Madame de Francueil (20 April, 1751) that it was her class, the class of the rich, that was responsible for his having had to abandon his children. With responsibility thus shifted from one's self to the rich, the next step is inevitable, namely to start a crusade against the members of a class which, without any warrant from "Nature," oppresses its brothers, the members of other classes, and forces them into transgression. A man may thus dodge his duties as a father, and at the same time pose as a paladin of humanity. Rousseau is very close here to our most recent agitators. . . .

. . . The essence of Rousseauistic as of other romance, I may repeat, is to be found not in any mere fact, not even in the fact of sensation, but in a certain quality of the imagination. Rousseauism is, it is true, an emancipation of impulse, especially of the impulse of sex. . . . But what one has even here, as the imagination grows increasingly romantic, is less the reality than the dream of the beautiful moment, an intensity that is achieved only in the tower of ivory. . . .

The atony and aridity of which the sufferer from romantic melancholy complains may have other sources besides the depression that follows upon the achieving of emotional intensity whether in revery or in fact; it may also be an incident in the warfare between head and heart that assumes so many forms among the spiritual posterity of Jean-Jacques. The Rousseauist seeks happiness in emotional spontaneity and this spontaneity seems to be killed by the head which stands aloof and dissects and analyzes. . . .

Whether the victim of romantic melancholy feels or analyzes he is equally incapable of action. He who faces resolutely the rude buffetings of the world is gradually hardened against them. The romantic movement is filled with the groans of those who have evaded action and at the same time become highly sensitive and highly self-conscious. . . .

When the romanticist is not posing as the victim of fate he poses as the victim of society. Both ways of dodging moral responsibility enter into the romantic legend of the *poète maudit*. Nobody loves a poet. His own mother, according to Baudelaire, utters a malediction upon him. That is because the poet feels so exquisitely that he is at once odious and unintelligible to the ordinary human pachyderm. Inasmuch as the philistine is not too sensitive to act he has a great advantage over the poet in the real world and often succeeds in driving him from it and indeed from the life itself.

This inferiority in action is a proof of the poet's ideality. . . . It is hardly necessary to say that great poets of the past have not been at war with their public in this way. The reason is that they were less taken up with the uttering of their own uniqueness; they were, without ceasing to be themselves, servants of the general sense. . . .

. . . The weakness of the romantic pursuit of novelty and wonder and in general of the philosophy of the beautiful moment — whether the erotic moment or the moment of cosmic revery — is that it does not reckon sufficiently with the something deep down in the human breast that craves the abiding. To pin one's hope to happiness to the fact that "the world is so full of a number of things" is an appropriate sentiment for a "Child's Garden of Verse." For the adult to maintain an exclusive Bergsonian interest in "the perpetual gushing forth of novelties" would seem to betray an inability to mature. The effect on a mature observer of an age so entirely turned from the One to the Many as that in which we are living must be that of a prodigious peripheral richness joined to a great central void. . . .

Intrinsic and Historic Romanticism

JACQUES BARZUN

Jacques Barzun, after a distinguished career as professor of history at
Columbia University, has become Provost of Columbia University. He has published copiously, as critic and editor, but much of his most significant work
has been in his studies in modern cultural history, especially in his biography
of Berlioz, his *Darwin, Marx, and Wagner*, and his *Classic Romantic and
Modern* (first published as *Romanticism and the Modern Ego*) from which the
following selection is drawn. While Barzun treats the problem of definition most
carefully, his definition itself involves explanation. It is notable how central
also is his concern for an evaluation of Romanticism which differs radically
from those of Saunders and Babbitt.

ROMANTICISM — DEAD OR ALIVE?

Romanticism is supposed to have died
over a century ago. The French date its
demise with false precision from the failure
of Victor Hugo's last produced play in
1843. Others make the knell sound earlier
or later, but the fact of death is rather
complacently taken for granted.

And yet if one opens other books, equally
reputable, and if one looks at the periodical
press devoted to politics and letters, one
finds that romanticism is considered still a
living threat. It is held plausible to say that
the "romantic view of life" is the enemy of
reason, science, and democracy. The Romantic writers from Byron, Carlyle, and
Goethe to their so-called neo-Romantic dis-
ciples, Nietzsche and William James, are
quoted and rebuked as inspirers of the
various totalitarian movements of this century. Rousseau is mauled from time to time
by intemperate journalists and Hegel credited with the feat of having turned Germany into a militarist people. Romanticism,
though "outgrown" and repudiated, seems
still to be a force in the battle of ideas.

We are thus faced at the outset with a
flat contradiction, which does not disap-
pear but deepens and spreads as we go
farther into the subject. Is romanticism
really dead? How can totalitarianism be a
"romantic" phenomenon when what we
most deplore (and try to imitate) is its so-
called political "realism"? How can the supposedly dreamy romantic individualists of
early nineteenth-century Germany be the
creators of the modern anti-individualistic
state? . . .

These are questions for the historian of
ideas. But Romanticism, as we just saw, is
not merely a topic for historians. It is a live
subject for this age of social and cultural
revolution and it poses practical questions:
Is Romanticism native to the human mind
or is it an aberration? If an aberration, what
are its symptoms and how can it be dealt
with? What likeness and difference are
there between Romanticism a hundred
years ago and Romanticism today? And if
neo-romanticism has been the enemy at the
gate since the nineties, what is the opposing
view or tradition to adopt and fight for as
our own?

All these questions take one thing for
granted — namely, that everybody knows
what romanticism is. The words "great romantics" or "German romantics" are used
as if their meaning were perfectly clear and

From *Classic Romantic and Modern* by Jacques Barzun, pp. 1–10, 13–17, 53–56, 58–60, 62–66,
78–81, 83–84, 91–92, 137–138, by permission of Little, Brown and Co., Atlantic Monthly Press.
Copyright © 1943, 1961 by Jacques Barzun.

agreed upon by everybody. That is the impression infallibly gathered from reading books. The truth is that at least half the contradictions come from the tolerated looseness in this use of the term "Romanticism." . . .

To find a core of fixed sense in "romantic" and "romanticism" requires that we consider certain common aspects of a great many subjects. The quest takes us from political and social history to critical facts about poetry, the arts, and philosophy; and thence to matters of psychology, religion, and common belief. . . .

. . . What I am about to discuss is not some vague literary and emotional outlook known as Romantic, but the meaning of a whole age as seen against the background of its close predecessor by yet a third age — our own. . . . Treated thus, Romanticism appears as something more than an isolated poetic movement in one country or another. It is a European phenomenon, occurring within certain historic dates and possessing certain characteristics.

If we wish to disinfect a word or an idea from casual and false associations, we begin by trying to define it. Unfortunately, definitions of romanticism already exist by the dozen and have remained without effect. One reason is that definition is not enough. We must also have a clear conception of the many proper uses to which a comprehensive term of this sort can be put. Because in the past many different things have been called romantic, some scholars have denied the possibility of giving a definition that will hold in all cases; or they have denied that romanticism stood for anything clear or solid. This is to play into the hands of the woolly-minded by suggesting that unless a word means one thing and one only, it can mean anything or nothing. . . .

Now "romantic" has two distinct fields of application. In one sense, it refers to human traits which may be exhibited at any time or place. In the second sense, it is a name given to a period in history because of the notable figures that gave it its peculiar character. These two meanings are obviously related. A period has a given character simply because at that time a human tendency is dominant. A Romantic, a Puritan, a Rationalist, a Pietist, are not separate zoological species, but recurring varieties of human beings, distinguished from one another by the relative value they place on certain attitudes. But this differentiation by means of dominant traits does not exclude the presence of others. The Rationalist is not the only man possessed of reason, nor are the Puritan and the Pietist devoid of it — any more than the Realist or the Romantic. When we call the eighteenth century the Age of Reason, we only mean an age when men talked a great deal about reason and hoped that its conscious use would bring about a marked improvement in human affairs. Only a hardened literalist supposes the name to imply that the eighteenth century had a monopoly of rationality and that before and after men were unreasoning or unreasonable.

With the word "romantic" it is this kind of false implication that gets in the way of its descriptive use. Few speakers or writers stop to check the applicability of the term by seeing how well it will cover other cases that deserve the name equally with the one they have chosen. . . . The difficulty of showing clear connections increases with each step that we take towards a more inclusive view. What actual relation is there between Keats's *Ode to a Nightingale* and *Mein Kampf,* or between Goya's etchings of the War of Liberation in Spain and the exploits of modern dictators in the same peninsula?

Usually, two ways are taken to evade this difficulty. One is to pick and choose among the romanticists those who are fancied to be "wholly" or "essentially" romantic — to choose a passage from Byron and drop out of sight all of Keats, Wordsworth, Shelley, Coleridge, and a hundred others. This is an admission of failure for any generality. Nor is it essentially different to say that only the German romantics are to blame for the new lawlessness. For, on that assumption, how did the dictators in other countries achieve *their* synthesis with no German tradition to aid them? And further, how is German romanticism different from the French, English, and Spanish kinds? The difference, if any, must be the source of the evil, and not the romanticism itself.

In other words, if we are committed to the view that an objectionable development in society is a new expression of historic romanticism, we must be able to show that most of the great men who lived a hundred and twenty-five years ago advocated or worked for that particular result. We must show that Goethe, Byron, Kant, Schiller, Carlyle, Emerson, Beethoven, Mickiewicz, Blake, Delacroix, Shelley, Schopenhauer, Heine, Berlioz, Pushkin, Scott, Dumas, Manzoni, Chopin, Lamb, Hazlitt, Thoreau, and perhaps a hundred other representative figures of the early nineteenth century, were pioneers of the totalitarian or welfare or other unwelcome kind of state. We can perhaps tolerate a few exceptions to the proposed generality, but obviously we cannot have more exceptions than cases in which the generality holds true.

The second way out of the impasse consists in saying that it is not in the romantics' expressed opinions or outward acts that we find the roots of militant tyranny. It is in the spirit underlying all romanticist work — whether it be a poem or a political theory. At this rate, Wordsworth's love of nature and Delacroix's love of a divided palette are equally dangerous to the future of democracy. On this same view, the liberal Byron and the conservative Sir Walter Scott were in the same party preparing the way for dictatorship. It was in them some secret but powerful germ which time has brought to full growth in the form of persecution and military imperialism.

This second hypothesis is no better than the first. It deals too much in abstraction, both when it talks about romanticism and when it reduces the transformations of modern societies to an advocacy of force and conquest. Indeed, the slightest ac-

quaintance with the mere bulk of the subject matter involved in this comparison shows the frivolity of the supposition. . . .

. . . I have deliberately tried to reproduce the existing confusion in order to break up the casual and one-sided, yet persistent, association between the notion of romanticism and the various imperialisms, internal and external, which are fathered upon it. Neither the gifted men of a century ago nor a hidden something in their make-up will directly account for our bad world. Leaving till later the question of a link between romanticism and modern collectivism, I go on now with the questions that this linkage has raised: Who are the romanticists and what is the common bond that makes them bear a common name?

In English, the noun "Romanticism" gives two adjectives — romantic and romanticist. They are not commonly differentiated, but it is to be desired that they should be. We should then be able to tell apart the two distinct fields of application I have begun to distinguish: romanticism as an historical movement and romanticism as a characteristic of human beings. We should then say: "My friend X is a romantic" and "the poet Byron is a romanti*cist*." When we say *the romanticists* at large we should mean a number of men who lived at a particular time and place, and who did certain things that fixed them in the mind of posterity. However much they differ ideally or fought among themselves, Byron, Wordsworth, Shelley, Victor Hugo, Leopardi, Mickiewicz, and Schiller were romanticists. They received the name whether they liked it or not. Indeed, many romanticists vigorously disclaimed the title, like Delacroix, or accepted it for only half their work, like Goethe. In this sense, romanticism is a mere tag and not an adequate description. You cannot infer a man's personal characteristics, much less his opinions, from his correct labeling as a romanticist. What you can infer, we shall shortly see. Meantime, think of romanticist as a term comparable to "Man of the Renaissance." . . .

With romanticism, the problem is complicated by the fact that during the romantic period small groups of writers or thinkers appropriated the general name to themselves. In Germany, for instance, scholars distinguish between Early and Late Romantic. But in neither of these groups will you find Schiller and Goethe. They stand apart, and yet Goethe's *Faust* is a bible of Romanticism. If you wish to find another German romanticist, Heine, you must look for him among the "Young Germany" group. This is the petty politics of cultural history. In French romanticism likewise, you will at one time find Victor Hugo and Stendhal on opposite sides, each representing a different shade of literary policy. In England, no one was called a Romanticist while living. All this is of great interest to the biographer or the historian of the several arts. But to use these temporary distinctions, as some have done, in order to blur the outlines of an era is to be guilty of obscurantism through pedantry. When the educated man has a true general conception of romanticism, it will be time to refine upon its details. For our present purpose, historic romanticism can be defined as comprising those Europeans whose birth falls between 1770 and 1815, and who achieved distinction in philosophy, statecraft, and the arts during the first half of the nineteenth century. . . .

We have then a group of men known as romanticists and living as contemporaries between 1770 and 1850. What, besides time, binds them together? It is at this point that we pass from *historic* romanticism to what may be called *intrinsic* romanticism. I have suggested that if an attitude becomes noticeable or dominant in a given period, its elements must be latent in human beings, or in certain human beings, all the time. In individual instances we call it this or that kind of temperament. . . . Not that each of these represents a fixed type; rather it is a combination of human traits which for one reason or another happens to be stressed, valued, cultivated at a given historical moment. Why one attitude

is preferred to another is something for the cultural historian to explain after the event, but *that* it is preferred is the reason for our being able to speak of a romantic period.

This distinction between *permanent* elements in human nature and their periodic emphasis in history is the first of the devices by which we can make more exact and serviceable our use of the name "romantic." If, for instance, we hear William James called a romantic, we are entitled to say: "James was not contemporary with Byron; what precisely have you in mind when you classify them under the same head?" If, as is likely, the answer given is: "I call him romantic because of his irrationalism," the field is then open to argument over the correctness of the description and over the propriety of making one belief or opinion taken at random symptomatic of a whole temperament or philosophy. The libraries are full of books, usually written in wartime, and which show that from Luther to Hitler, or from Fichte to Mussolini, or from Rousseau to Stalin "one increasing purpose runs." The demonstration is made by stringing together on one line of development all thinkers who "believe in the will" or "believe in hero worship" or "believe in the divine right of the people." In these works the intention of human ideas is disregarded for the sake of finding a collection of scapegoats.

The history of ideas cannot be written so, like an invoice of standardized goods. It is a subject requiring infinite tact. On the one hand, diversity must be reduced to clear patterns for the sake of intelligibility; on the other, the meaning of each idea must be preserved from falsification by constant reference to its place and purport in history. It is strictly meaningless to speak of someone as "a believer in a strong state" — strong for what, for whom, by what means, against whom? . . .

At this point I may state dogmatically what I shall show in the sequel, that romanticism is not equivalent to irrationalism, nor sentimentality, nor individualism, nor collectivism, nor utopian aspirations, nor love, nor hate, nor indolence, nor feeble-mindedness. Consequently if any of these human traits particularly excite one's disapproval one must call them by their proper names, and not shirk responsibility for the judgment by terming their manifestations "romantic." . . .

. . . Romanticism is not a return to the Middle Ages, a love of the exotic, a revolt from Reason, an exaggeration of individualism, a liberation of the unconscious, a reaction against scientific method, a revival of pantheism, idealism and catholicism, a rejection of artistic conventions, a preference for emotion, a movement back to nature, or a glorification of force. Nor is it any of a dozen more generalities which have been advanced as affording the proper test. It is not any of these things for the simple reason that none of them can be found uniformly distributed among the great romanticists. Mention any such characteristic and a contrary-minded critic will name you a Romanticist who did not possess it; he may even produce one who clearly strove for the opposite. It is this truth that has led a number of critics to abandon the search — and to abuse romanticism all the more for not yielding up its secret on first inspection.

This is not to say that many of the tendencies enumerated in the textbooks were not present in the romantic age. They obviously were, and it is in romantic work that scholars have found them. But a collection of features defines nothing unless it is common to nearly all the individuals examined. The error has consisted in supposing that what unites an age are common opinions and common traits. If this were true what would become of the war of opinions which characterizes every age? . . .

In other words, what we want as a definition of intrinsic romanticism is the thing that gave rise to — and that incidentally explains — all the other attitudes I have enumerated. Why did some romanticists attack Reason, why did some turn catholic, why were some liberal, others reactionary? Why did some praise the Middle Ages and others adore the Greeks? Clearly, the one thing that unifies men in a given age is not their individual philosophies but the dominant problem that these philosophies are designed to solve. In the romantic period, as will appear, this problem was to create a new world on the ruins of the old. The French Revolution and Napoleon had made a clean sweep. Even before the Revolution, which may be taken as the outward sign of an inward decay, it was no longer possible to think, act, write, or paint as if the old forms still had life. The critical philosophers of the eighteenth century had destroyed their own dwelling place. The next generation must build or perish. Whence we conclude that romanticism is first of all constructive and creative; it is what may be called a solving epoch, as against the *dissolving* eighteenth century.

Because the problem of reconstruction was visible to many men does not mean that they all proposed the same solution, or saw all its aspects in the same way. The divergences were due to differences of temperament, geographical situation, and special interest. A poet such as Wordsworth or Victor Hugo saw the emptiness of eighteenth-century diction and the need of creating a new vocabulary for poetry; a philosopher such as Schopenhauer saw the illusoriness of eighteenth-century hopes of progress and the need of recharting moral reality, with suggestions for better enduring it; a political theorist like Burke, who apprehended the wholesale destruction of the social order, had to propose an alternative means of change; a thinker like Hegel, who was at once philosopher, political theorist, and esthetician, saw creation as the result of conflict in history and in the mind, and proposed nothing less than a new logic to explain the nature of change. He then showed how to use it for rebuilding on more lasting premises.

These men clearly cannot be made into

a romantic *school,* but they equally clearly partake of a romanticist *temper.* More than that, they share certain broad predilections in common, such as the admiration for energy, moral enthusiasm, and original genius. It is because an era faces one dominant problem in varying ways that certain human traits come to be held in greater esteem than they were before. The task of reconstruction manifestly does demand energy, morality, and genius, so that the new passion for them was thus not a whimsical or useless trait in the romantics, but a necessity of their position.

By the same logic, one is led to see that romanticism was far from being an escape from reality on the part of feeble spirits who could not stand it. The truth is that these spirits wanted to change the portions of reality that they did not like, and at least record their ideals when the particular piece of reality would not yield — both these being indispensable steps toward reconstruction. . . .

But, it may be said, other periods faced with the task of creation have not produced cultures resembling romanticism. The very system which preceded romanticism and came to an end with the eighteenth century was created around 1650 and it took the form that we call classical. True enough; so to understand romanticism we must add to the fact of its creative mission the further fact that it conceived its mission in a certain way. It conceived it in the light of a great contradiction concerning man. I mean the contrast between man's greatness and man's wretchedness; man's power and man's misery. . . .

But in a thinking reed, as Pascal terms man, the contradictory state of having powers and of feeling one's weakness is not one to be dumbly endured. Some resolution must be found even while the protective social order is being built. Indeed, many men feel that the imperfect social order is inadequate to resolve the inner conflict. Hence the search for a philosophy, a religion, a faith, which will transcend and unify the felt disharmony. Pascal himself, as we know, found this faith in ascetic Christianity. The romanticists, a hundred and fifty years after Pascal, found it in many different objects of belief — pantheism, Catholicism, socialism, vitalism, art, science, the national state. To fill out the list would be to give a catalogue of the contributions of romanticism. What matters here is the interconnection of all these faiths through their roots in the double problem of making a new world and making it in the knowledge that man is both creative and limited, a doer and a sufferer, infinite in spirit and finite in action. . . .

THE CLASSIC OBJECTION

. . . In the eighteenth century, the most perfect of neo-classical ages, the stirrings of unchanneled emotion were the most tangible force disrupting the old order. No sooner had "civilization" reached its high point, as all agreed, than restlessness set in and the South Sea islands began to seem a better world. Throughout Europe new interests developed — in popular ballads, in Gothic architecture, in natural scenery, in sentimental stories, in informal gardens, in tales of horror and mystery, in the Celtic and Germanic literatures as against the Graeco-Roman — all having the common feature of a pleasing *ir*regularity. . . .

The significant fact is that the new taste was for pleasing irregularity. Each innovation was just another fad, but all together amounted to a shift in outlook. The results were to mark an epoch not only in art and society, but in political forms and natural science. What happened in these four realms may be summed up in the words which apply particularly to science: it was a Biological Revolution. The term says plainly enough that the absolute reign of physics and mathematics was over, and with it the dominance of the Reason patterned upon these two sciences. By the end of the eighteenth century new branches of knowledge — the sciences of man — had come of age: anthropology, ethnology, and zoology were offering new facts, new analogies, new modes of thought. Cartesian and Newtonian mechanics were taken for granted; the new principle was vitalism and the new theory, evolution. The mechanical materialism which had threatened to overcome all rival philosophies was in full retreat. . . .

. . . What does biology imply that mechanics does not? It implies that life is an element and not merely a combination of dead parts. It implies organic structure and organic function. It implies that the primary reality is the individual and not either the parts of which he is made or the artificial groupings which he may enter into. This is, in a word, individualism. Within the individual, the motive power is, as its name reveals, emotion. Consciousness and intelligence remain at the top of the hierarchy of values but they are not disembodied or centered upon themselves. They serve larger interests, which are those of life itself — the survival of the individual and of the species.

Survival in turn suggests that the first law of the universe is not thought but action. As Goethe has Faust say, "In the beginning was" — not the Word, or Thought, but "the Deed." Action means effort, energy, possibly strife and certainly risk. The world is a world of novelty, in which changing situations cannot always be met by rules previously learned, though imagination can foresee and forearm the creature, who thereby becomes also an agent of creation. But imagination and creation carry with them no guarantee of success. The sustaining principle in man and his new world is therefore not reason — which is merely the already acquired and codified experience — but faith, which is hope plus the power of hope to realize itself. . . .

. . . To the romanticist, religion is no longer a superstition or a bald statement that the universe must have a First Cause; religion is an intellectual and emotional necessity. As Pascal said, man must wager on the existence of God, "because he is embarked." In the romantic period, man wagered on the existence of the Catholic or Protestant God, on pantheism, on art, on science, on the national state, on the future of mankind: but in all the pattern is the same. The solutions differ in concrete particulars only because salvation is ultimately individual.

With these premises, classicism — at least in its old form — cannot subsist. It had built a shelter for man on too narrow an enclosure. It had supposed society to be static, emotions compressible, and novelty needless. It had selected what seemed to it best and truest and most eternal — monarchy, orthodoxy, courtly etiquette, mathematics, and rules of art and of morality so simple that their universality could be deemed self-evident. But what had it selected these elements from? Clearly from a previous romanticism, that of the sixteenth-century Renaissance, an age of exploration and creation. . . .

ROMANTIC ART

An historical review of the classical epoch nearest to us has enabled us to measure the distance between its ideal of peace and serenity and its actual tendencies toward repression and formalism. The psychological presuppositions of that age naturally threw light on the differences between rationalist and romanticist; differences which, speaking figuratively, correspond to the difference between physics and biology. This contrast faces, as it were, backwards from the nineteenth century to the eighteenth and seventeenth. A second usual contrast, that between romanticist and realist, presumably looks forward to a movement later than romanticism. Since these terms belong first of all to the realm of art, I want now to argue against this postponement of the realistic label and to suggest that, on the evidence just set forth, romanticism is realism.

If this is too great a shock to common usage let it be softened by a modification of the ideas behind each term. By the equation romanticism = realism I do not mean that there is no difference between romanticism and the artistic movement known after 1850 as Realism. . . . What I am concerned with here is to show that what the romanticists of the period 1790 to 1850 sought and found was not a dream world into which to escape, but a real world in which to live. The exploration of reality was the fundamental intention of romantic art.

Before we come to particulars, the general setting may be put in a few words: classicism perished from an excess of abstraction and generality. This was most visibly true in the several arts, and nothing shows more clearly the romanticists' realistic purpose than their refusal to go on imitating forms whose contents had evaporated. Seeing this refusal, we believe too readily in the miscalled "romantic revolt." We imagine a sudden and irresponsible rebellion of brash young men against the wisdom and experience of their elders. It was nothing of the kind. The breaking away was reluctant, painful, and deliberate. After much soul-searching and abortive efforts to continue in traditional ways, a whole generation of talents came to see that to write or paint in the manner of Pye, Gottsched, and Delille, of David and Reynolds, was no longer possible.

There was no choice but to begin afresh. The romanticist was in the position of a primitive with the seven arts to create out of nothing. At the same time, he labored under the handicap of having "inimitable" classical masterpieces held up to him to imitate, even though the substance of these great works had already been rendered threadbare by repetition and refinement. The romantic revolt consisted solely in refusing to do the undoable.

Having perforce given up conventional abstractions, clichés, poetic diction, and classical rules, what did the romanticists turn to? The answer can be generalized: for substance they turned to the world about and within them; they tried to meet the claims of every existing reality, both internal and external. For form, they relied on earlier romantic periods and on their own inventive genius.

The characteristics of romanticism which the textbooks list as if they were arbitrary choices by eccentric artists are merely the embodiment of what I have just said. As against poetic diction and "noble" words, the romanticists admitted all words; as against the exclusive use of a selected Graeco-Roman mythology, they took in the Celtic and Germanic; as against the uniform setting and tone of classical tragedy, they studied and reproduced the observable diversities known as "local color." As against the antique subjects and the set scale of pictorial merits prescribed by the Academy, they took in the whole world, seen and unseen, and the whole range of colors. As against the academic rules prohibiting the use of certain chords, tonalities, and modulations, they sought to use and give shape to all manageable combinations of sound. As against the assumption that no civilization had existed since the fall of Rome, they rediscovered the Middle Ages and the sixteenth century and made history their dominant avocation. As against the provincial belief that Paris and London were the sole centers of human culture, they traveled to such remote places as America and the Near East and earned the name of "exotic" for their pains. As against the idea that the products of cosmopolitan sophistication afford the only subjects worth treating, they began to treasure folk literature and folk music and to draw the matter of their art from every class and condition of men. As against the materialistic view that only the tangible exists, they made room in their notion of reality for the world of dreams, the ineffable in man and nature, and the supernatural.

All this they did knowingly, deliberately, with the patience and tenacity of pioneers and explorers. Hence to the scoffer who would. dismiss the "romantic revolt" one must reply as Liancourt did to Louis XVI: "Sire, it is a revolution." . . .

As a body, there has never been a group . . . more persistently curious of fact than the romantic artists. The greater part of their poetry was the record of observation, whether of their own souls or of the world outside. The accuracy is sometimes painful and the detail excessive. But there have been few see-ers and reporters as minute and comprehensive as Wordsworth, Balzac, Hazlitt, Goethe, Victor Hugo, and Stendhal. One may not enjoy what they saw or approve what they said of it, but wherever one begins looking for the "authority" behind their reports one is likely to find some actual and factual experience.

What is true of the poets is, *a fortiori,* true of the painters. . . .

Whatever one may think of the results achieved, it is a fact beyond dispute that the romantic artists worked like scientific researchers. Their notebooks, their critical writings, their letters and treatises on composition are there to testify that technique was to them as important as subject matter. Indeed they reasserted the old truth that the distinction between the two is one for the critic rather than the creator. The artist has said nothing until he has found the right form. Accordingly, form, or rather forms, preoccupied the romanticists to a degree we hardly recognize now that for a hundred years we have used their discoveries and inventions. We have come to think of them as ready-made for their makers as they have been for us. A volume on each of the arts and one on each of the European nations would not suffice to discuss the successful creation or adaptation of forms by the romantic artists. Let anyone conversant with poetry imagine English poetry without the forms bequeathed by Wordsworth; French poetry without Victor Hugo; German without Goethe. And in their obsession with variety, as close examination shows, the romantics acted not merely as innovators and revolutionists but as great restorers and wise conservatives. . . .

The attempt to reconcile experimental fact with spiritual truth may in fact be the reason why romanticism has been falsely interpreted as the enemy of science. Both the romantic philosopher and the romantic artist agree in thinking science valuable, but they clearly perceive that science can

deal only with a restricted field of experience. Scientific method proceeds by exclusion and achieves wonderful results; art and philosophy are, on the contrary, inclusive disciplines — none more so than romantic philosophy and romantic art. This is the point of the romanticist attack, not on science, but on materialism: materialism narrows down the universe to a fraction of itself. The romanticists were realists precisely because they admitted the widest possible range of experience as real. They made mistakes as to particular facts, for they were fallible men, but they made no mistake as to the endless variety of things that are. Their critics cannot have it both ways: the romanticists' "thirst for experience," which is condemned as a dispersion of effort, is at least a proof that phenomena as such were to them of infinite concern. . . .

ROMANTIC LIFE

Romantic art, then, is not "romantic" in the vulgar sense, but "realistic" in the sense of concrete, full of particulars, and thus congenial to the inquiring spirit of history and science. Romanticism is not simply a synonym for subjectivism, overexpressiveness, or sentimentality, though when strictly understood these terms suggest respectively the philosophy, the technique, and the inherited accident of romantic esthetics. Can it be that "romantic" meaning "wild and foolish" applies exclusively to a way of life? . . .

But what is a romantic life? An answer lurks in the influence of Napoleon's example upon the men of the romanticist generation. Though there are notable exceptions, it is astonishing how many diverse minds of the first rank were caught in the Napoleonic spell. Beethoven, Goethe, Byron, Scott, Hazlitt, Stendhal, Victor Hugo, Chateaubriand, Vigny, Manzoni, Mickiewicz, Foscolo, Balzac, are a few whose opinions on the subject are copious enough to show us the depth and discrimination of their regard. Napoleon was tyrant, conqueror, and faithless usurper — this the romanticist knew and said with absolute frankness. They condemned his destruction of liberty, his mania for war, and his open contempt for morality, but they found him nevertheless an indispensable symbol. He objectified one of their sensations: they used him as a shorthand sign of what they meant by genius and energy. . . .

Out of admiration for him grew the wider attitude that has been called the "cult of energy." In its worst aspects it could of course become mere waste motion or violence. It could be destructive of the individual, as in the career of Julien Sorel in Stendhal's *The Red and the Black;* or demoralizing, as in Balzac's insatiable heroes; no doubt the age devoured its men. But we must not forget that when we speak of the romantic life we mean a model held up primarily to men with the requisite balance of gifts for art or public life. If we apply the test of fruits to both these groups during the romantic period, we find that "romantic energy" is no vain phrase. Energy was not merely a cult but a fact. Whatever we may think of its products, the products are there in abundance. The labors of Scott are legendary but true, so are those of Balzac. The historical, editorial, and political work of Guizot, of Gentz, of Macaulay; the threefold career of Goethe; the nine hundred canvasses of Delacroix — not counting his murals; the patience of Blake, the incredible output of Turner; the herculean activity of a Weber, Berlioz, Paganini, or Liszt in creating a new musical world — all this means work if it means nothing else. . . .

Meantime we need not be surprised that the romantic life was robust and productive, because, as we know, the romanticists were stimulated, pressed onward, justified by extraordinary events. The French Revolution and Napoleon had, in Stendhal's phrase, made a clean slate. But this stimulation was purely spiritual. No one was waiting with open arms to receive their gifts. One has but to read the lifelong complaints of Goethe — a relatively fortunate man as well as a stoical mind — to see that

the energetic life had to be lived in a dampening milieu. For the habits of individual men change at unequal rates, and when it seemed to the young Goethe or Schiller "impossible" to go on turning out literature in the manner of their predecessors, it seemed to the good burghers not only possible but desirable that this should be done.

This state of affairs explains why we associate the struggle of the artist against his environment with the romantic period. . . . In the nineteenth century, the artist starved just as much as in the eighteenth, but at least he made his grievance known, he analyzed the general conditions that made it representative, and he fought society's instinctive attempts to muzzle him. It is this rhythm of repulse and counterattack which lends to the lives of so many romanticists that defiant and assertive character which in looking back we mistake for egotism or misanthropic sulks.

But as we have just seen, the issues the romanticists fought for were larger than their personal selves. They were political, social, and esthetic issues. . . .

The romantics' nationalism is cultural . . . nationalism. They spoke less of nations than of "peoples," whom they considered the creators and repositories of distinct cultures. The romantics could hardly have overlooked popular cultures and remained good historians, or even good critics. But they went further and maintained that each human group, being a unique product of history, was worth preserving in its integrity. They compared Europe to a bouquet, each flower growing in its appointed soil, a simile which only slowly degenerated into the racial absolutism of blood and fatherland. . . .

Modern critics of romanticism are prone to assert that out of this doctrine grew present-day mysticisms about nation and *Volk.* This outcome, they add, was all the more natural because the romantics preached the struggle for life — an idea, they go on, which is not only included in the Faustian myth but is a part of the biological view of man which twice in our century German imperialism has exploited.

This implication of descent is plausible but not true. By hurrying over the points of contact between one idea and the next it shows as inevitable and universal what was in fact only local and possible. We saw earlier how the peculiar condition of Germany under the Napoleonic tyranny put a premium upon aggressive energy. This energy developed around the idea of the state and was re-enforced by that of a nation united through its common culture. At this stage it was indeed cultural nationalism militant — but militant in defense. Even so, it was not a unanimous feeling. . . .

Let me, for convenience rather than emphasis, recapitulate what I believe to be tenable and instructive about the great movement just coming to an end. The romantic era in Europe produced two generations of men who attempted, between 1780 and 1850, a feat of cultural renovation. The classical order, dying of overabstraction and false generality, had been devoured by its own children, the Enlightened philosophers. Political revolution and Napoleonic dictatorship buried the past and leveled the ground. The romanticists had the task of reconstruction. The vast horizons opened up by war and social upheaval gave romanticism its scope: it was inclusive, impatient of barriers, eager for diversity. It treasured fact and respected the individual as a source of fact. Accordingly, its political philosophy was an attempt to reconcile personal freedom with the inescapable need of collective action. Rousseau, Burke, Kant, Hegel, agreeing on the nature of the problem, differed only in lesser particulars. They were not anarchists or imperialists, but theorists of equilibrium in motion.

Alive to diversity, romanticism bound up patriotism with the life of peoples and gave form to a cultural nationalism compatible with international amity. Observant and imaginative, it rediscovered history and gave an impulse to the arts which has not yet died out. True to its inclusive purpose, romantic art was simultaneously idealistic, realistic, and symbolic; impressionist, expressionist, and surrealist. It produced forms and amassed contents only now nearing exhaustion, after furnishing the models for the movements which we enumerate through the past century as Realism, Symbolism, Impressionism, Naturalism, and Post-Impressionism.

The men who carried out this cultural revolution were both fortunate and ill-fated. Coming first after the deluge, they had the luck of position. They could and did infinitely more than it was given to their successors to do. Yet being men, not demigods, they often groaned and sometimes broke under the burden of their responsibility. Astounding in their energy, production, inventiveness, and moral fervor, they also found within themselves traits that led them to proclaim man both strong and weak. Their melancholy sense of failure and love of death; their recourse to opiates and stimulants; the retreat of some of their number to traditional havens, alike prove that their lot was tragic. The best of them are in fact like heroes of tragedy in that they simultaneously fail and triumph, irritate and impress us. They are out of scale with the common crowd and we can neither take them to our bosoms nor let them alone.

Though we cannot forget them, their lives were more arduous and more subtly organized than we remember. The striking generalities of the textbook writer about romantic careers are falser than most critical commonplaces, because the roles filled by the romantics are open only once in every century or two, and there clings something of the incredible to such human destinies. Moreover, in virtue of its very largeness and variety, romanticism is bound to seem vulnerable and loose. Whereas, to topple a classic orthodoxy, people must risk their lives to undermine it in secret, a romanticist position is breached at once by anyone who wants to tidy up the world by enforcing a few simple rules. Whereas the classical temper can be individually indulged within the romantic order, the contrary is impossible. But men's unstillable fear of diversity and impatience with failure are ever at work, and to them romanticism sooner or later succumbs. The age of Realism begins, and seeks to base a new convention on materialism. This is what happened in Europe around 1850. But its limitations soon generated a counter-reaction, a neo-romanticism, appearing as Symbolism, Naturalism, and Impressionism.

Components of Romanticism

HOWARD E. HUGO

Professor Howard E. Hugo is associate professor of English at the University of California, Berkeley. In the introduction to *The Romantic Reader* he distinguishes six major areas of experience for which he defines the Romantic position. He imbeds in his discussion an effort to explain, in both intellectual and social terms, the appearance of the attitudes he distinguishes.

WE know that something happened from the late eighteenth century through the first half of the nineteenth to shatter a fairly homogeneous pattern of ideas, attitudes, behavior, and expression. In his introduction to the Viking Portable *Reader* that deals with the earlier period, Mr. Crane Brinton has eloquently pointed out the dangers of oversimplifying the Age of Reason. It too was an age containing diversities as varied as those we tend to attribute to the Romantics, with their principle of extreme individuation. Still, the range of feelings engendered by reason (and by its poor cousin, reasonableness) possessed a vague consistency. In praising reason the men of that age found a convenient way of uniting the highest aspirations of the human intellect with basic common sense and prudential activity.

The Romantic movement never possessed even this fuzzy unity. We speak more frequently of a movement, in the case of the Romantics, than of an "age" or "period," perhaps because our terminology is unconsciously influenced by Romantic rhetoric. All periods are really movements in time; but the exponents of Romanticism seemed unusually aware that theirs was a moment of flux, of organic change and growth, while they undertook to revolt against what they regarded as the fixed, outworn canons of preceding generations. Add to this deliberate choice of the organic, or changing, or illogical, an equally calculated desire of the Romantics to abandon uniformity — "I am not made like anyone I have ever met; I even venture to believe that I am not made like anyone now alive," announces Rousseau at the beginning of his *Confessions* — and the task of exact or complete definition becomes almost impossible. The quotations in the Prologue to this volume indicate how currents, cross-currents, and minor eddies obscured the direction of the tide. Partisans and detractors crossed party lines with baffling rapidity.

In all truth there were few individuals, . . . who thought of themselves as Romantics (whereas many audacious men of letters in the eighteenth century had been convinced that they represented an age of reason or an enlightenment). A small group of German intellectuals and artists living around Jena in 1800 were the first to exhibit glimmerings of Romantic self-consciousness. Although the English Lake poets — Wordsworth, Southey, and Coleridge — embraced a common literary cause at about the same date, they were not allied to the Lake District and hence to one another until some years after most of their most representative poetry had been written. In the 1820s and 1830s Paris abounded with *cénacles* and salons where the leading young artists congregated. At that time the members were aware of mutual bonds created by artistic rebellion and occasional political allegiances, but it was not until decades later that Hugo and Gautier would talk in restrospect of their youthful Romanticism. . . .

Somehow a lowest common denominator, perhaps tiny in magnitude, was shared by all. . . . Whatever Romanticism was we may best observe by seeing how its practitioners felt about six major areas of experience: the passions that move men, the heroic types in which the movement invested its sympathy, the past, the world and nature apart from man's achievements, revolt and reform, and the artist and his vocation.

THE MAN OF FEELING

The Enlightenment, that climax to the Age of Reason, had underscored the idea that all the major phases of experience fell into rational schemes comprehensible to the human mind. Man was no doubt irrational. One need only read Swift or Voltaire to catch the despair these keen intellects felt about human shortcomings. Yet rationality was the aim; and for them and less brilliant contemporaries those parts of the psyche related to the feelings and the passions were not relevant when ultimate values were at stake. If laws about the cosmos, society, the arts, and the nature of man were ever to be established, these had to be rules intelligible to the mind and to common sense.

How can we account for the reaction against such a beautiful rationalism that developed during the Romantic movement? Perhaps the eighteenth century flew too high, and those who claimed the highest place for reason inadvertently disclosed its final limits and possible inadequacy. To watch the progress of the eighteenth century is to observe the gradual intrusion of such terms as intuition, inspiration, taste, the moral sense, sensibility, and to note

their slow victory over a drier vocabulary. It would be foolish to assert that men suddenly started feeling and stopped thinking. At the same time one cannot deny that *feeling* came to take on dimensions hitherto ignored or minimized.

To this strange triumph the contributions were various. Intuitive processes are always private and yet universal, the property of all men despite superficial differences in rank, station, education, and mental abilities. The Age of Reason had discovered its ideal in the philosopher-gentleman who represented a kind of modern equivalent of Plato's philosopher-king. But with the rise of the middle class, both the social status and the learning and cultivation enjoyed by the gentleman meant less and less to the young man in search of a better world. Thus the real Rousseau, the fictional Werther and Harley (*The Man of Feeling*), all share at least two traits: acute emotional sensibility, which raises them above their less sensitive brothers, and an awareness of not belonging to the existing social order. The former trait took on many later configurations and names as the *philosophe* turned into the solitary dreamer: spleen, melancholy, the blue devils, *Weltschmerz, le mal du siècle*. What the Middle Ages had labeled acedia, the grave sin of spiritual sloth and despair, came to be the mark of spiritual distinction — a prerequisite for the genius, a necessity for the man of fashion. And when the social revolutions of 1789, 1830, and 1848 destroyed old orders only to create new systems for the organization of men, the same individuals were left to contemplate the ashes of their hopes — they for whom these same cataclysms had once seemed promises of liberation and fulfillment.

The Romantic man of feeling dwelt in a world of emotions where sadness predominated over happiness. Here he ramified the eighteenth-century cult of sensibility and diverted it into a single mournful channel. Laurence Sterne, writing his praise of "dear sensibility" in *A Sentimental Journey* (1768), showed that all experiences, pleasurable and painful, could be enriched when the heart was free to pour out tears or laughter. The Romantics strove to prove that sensibility was not equated with happiness. The Romantic *isolato* rarely laughed; if he did, it was after the manner of Byron: "And if I laugh at any mortal thing, / 'Tis that I may not weep." The wry smile covers up the catch in the throat and the incipient sob. . . .

. . . When Mme. de Staël introduced German literature to her French readers shortly after the turn of the century, one of her attacks on the proponents of the Enlightenment was their insufficient recognition of the charms and the reality of love. She extolled the Age of Chivalry less for its heroic aspects than for a manifestation of love as material for serious literature. It was time to turn once more to the gentler qualities of man's sexual instincts. . . .

. . . The Romantics suggested, as had Dante, that love was a route by which the time-bound individual might learn a vision of ultimate truth, a glimpse of that world which stands behind or above our meager existences. Hence love was a state of being that was eagerly to be coveted, not for purposes of physical satisfaction, but rather because the attraction of one soul for another was a guarantee that the entire universe was permeated with similar energy and spirit. . . .

THE ROMANTIC HERO

I want a hero: an uncommon want,
   When every year and month sends forth
    a new one,
Till, after cloying thè gazettes with cant,
   The age discovers he is not the true
    one.

Byron's lines from *Don Juan* are cogent and ironic when we remember that he created several impressive Romantic heroes (Childe Harold, Manfred, Don Juan) and that the legend he left behind him gave posterity still another. Taine once observed that every epoch tries to locate its particu-

lar "ruling personage" or "notable character," the figure that "contemporaries invest with their admiration and sympathy," in short, the hero. . . . From ancient times to our own the social leveling of the hero is relatively easy to discern. The captains and the kings depart. Shakespeare's King Lear (1606) is transformed into Balzac's retired noodle manufacturer, Père Goriot (1834), and subsequently into Willy Loman, hero of Arthur Miller's *Death of a Salesman* (1949). Democratization, the emphasis on egalitarian similarities between men rather than on their distinguishing differences, has made the hero increasingly difficult to define.

Voltaire once dryly commented, "I don't like heroes; they make too much noise." The Age of Reason was rationally unsympathetic to individuals who threatened to burst the confines of an orderly society, whether they were real or fictive. The rapier carried by the Renaissance courtier became the small-sword decoratively worn by the eighteenth-century nobleman on ceremonial occasions. What better emblem could stand for the decline of the hero as a fighting man? Both the Chesterfieldian gentleman and the honest, upright tradesman came to serve as models — one for the aristocracy, the other for the *bourgeoisie*. They fulfilled Voltaire's demand for essentially quiet types.

The developments conspiring to disrupt such relative passivity were various. We single out two. The sheer stress on individualism led to an increasing preoccupation with uniqueness, and hence to a weakening of the conviction that men resembled each other or that such solidarity was ultimately to be desired. A second development of the years following 1789 was the near-total destruction of aristocratic molds, which were never again to be repaired. Social disruption created a new class of young men released from ancient and restricting social hierarchies, each one of them — insofar as he realized his condition — anxious to find the career open to his talents.

The phrase reminds us of the meteoric

rise of the man who seemed to prove that the hero was not dead: Napoleon. His success, even his final defeat, became a paradigm and pattern for those whose aspirations were nonmilitary. . . . In an age of secularity the imitation of Napoleon rivaled any divine antecedent. Through Napoleon, Romanticism discovered a quality — greatness and genius or contrariwise he proved an hypothesis already current. That the decisions of men in a position of power could alter events was nothing new, but the phenomenon of Napoleon transcended the acts of his predecessors. No wonder that philosophers of history, Hegel the foremost, used him as an example of the great man who momentarily embodies the world spirit at certain crucial turning points.

The assertion of greatness and genius carries with it credentials of isolation and suffering. The albatross portrayed in Baudelaire's poem is sublimely beautiful only when it soars alone in the sky. On deck among ordinary humanity it becomes a figure of fun. The destiny of the genius, as Romantic generations found, is to be annihilated by the very society whose goals he has helped to reach, whose hopes he has articulated. The messiah becomes the outlaw, the scapegoat, the outsider. The necessary egotism of the Romantic hero may be capable of sustaining him temporarily. At the end he must go down before the collective onslaughts of his fellowmen. Perhaps here is a distinguishing feature of all Romantic heroes. The hero of the Greek epic, the mediaeval knight and *preux chevalier,* and the Renaissance aristocrat with his scholar's learning and courtier's ease — all were ideals created by societies in which the major metaphysical, social, and psychological premises were shared by everyone. The Romantic heroes lived their lives when traditional beliefs about the nature of the cosmos on one level, the organization and community of men on another, were brought to question. Even the contours of the mind seemed no longer to follow the intellectual pattern which the Age of Reason thought it discerned. Locke's *tabula rasa,* that blank slate upon which sense impressions are subsequently inscribed, is a far cry from the deep abysses of the soul or the irrational world of dreams into which we plunge with Poe, Novalis, Melville, and Coleridge. . . .

THE ROMANCE OF THE PAST

In the Romantic period, the past was revisited with a new zeal and necessity. One such return was to the world that neoclassicism had marked out for its own, the ancient world of Greece and Rome. The other was unique in that on the whole the Age of Reason had ignored the Middle Ages (the adjective "Dark" is indicative of Enlightenment attitudes toward Europe between the fall of Rome and the rise of New Learning) and the misty regions of the pagan and early Christian North. These were felt not to be separate cultures; they were not cultures in a strict sense at all. . . .

First consider pagan antiquity. The Greek gods never died. Ancient Greece has reinvigorated the thought of every epoch, although there were times when the light from Hellas seemed to burn low, as during the first ten centuries after Christ. The neo-classicism we associate with a portion of the Age of Reason was aware of its debt to the past. What then was Romantic Hellenism? How did it differ from its predecessor?

Perhaps it was less a difference than an intensification, when more information about classical civilization was revealed. . . .

. . . Gradually it became evident that the Romantic Hellenists sought to find a canonical civilization in Greece; an age of total social, political, moral, and aesthetic perfection such as the most ardent neoclassicist never dreamed; an imaginary kingdom and an Arcadia where hearts troubled by the present might seek nourishment from the glorious past. . . .

More radical was the slow revelation of another tradition — that of the Celtic, Scandinavian, Teutonic North, which existed in polar relation to the Mediterranean. We may be puzzled by the popularity of MacPherson's Ossianic poems, but we cannot ignore the hold these gloomy verses of doubtful authenticity had on Goethe, Byron, and Napoleon, not to mention thousands of less famous readers. Their melancholy and elegiac tone struck responsive chords in hearts already attuned to sweet sensibility. They spoke of an age that seemed morally superior and nationally closer to modern Europe than was Greece. Historians discovered information about societies long forgotten; Scandinavian mythology produced a pantheon of gods as various as Zeus's family. Poets wrote translations and imitations of the Norse *Eddas* and the tales and songs of the Nibelungs — those works in which ancient Celts, Saxons, Teutons, Vikings, and Northmen warred as strenuously and poetically as ever the Greeks and Trojans. And the disparate races were placed under the convenient heading of "Gothic."

This was mainly a pagan world existing during the first five or six centuries after Christ. The greater gap to be filled belonged to the high Middle Ages, with which the Gothic also came to be identified. When Gibbon said, "The schools of Oxford and Cambridge were founded in a dark age of false and barbarous science," his words expressed the attitude of the Age of Reason toward those times that stood between modern man and classical antiquity. By the close of the eighteenth century, however, such patronizing language was no longer the fashion. Nationalism was replacing cosmopolitanism; the *citoyen du monde* of the Enlightenment was giving way to the German, French, or English patriot; and the roots of a national past were located not in Greece and Rome — except for the Greeks and Italians — but in the days of Richard Coeur de Lion, Friedrick Barbarossa, Louis XI, and Robert the Bruce.

Moreover, philosophic and religious developments played important roles in what might otherwise seem an artistic, literary change of interest. Those for whom the light of reason shone brightest were chiefly deists — believers in some sort of God, but a God who resembled an impersonal cosmic clockmaker, the prime mover of Newton's universe. Some rationalists went further in the direction of philosophical skepticism. But one feels both deism and skepticism to be played out for many intellectuals by 1800. (Naturally there always had been practicing Protestants and Catholics; we speak of the extremes.) A definite Christian revival took place in all quarters, spurred on when the excesses of the French Revolution and its aftermath were interpreted by many as the logical, horrifying outcome of secular and "enlightened" thought. Novalis, Burke, Chateaubriand, and Coleridge compose a curious group. Whether they talked of cathedrals or conservatism in church and state, of tradition, loyalty, or duty, they pleaded for a return to Christian principles and thus represented a movement of which the Gothic revival was both a product and a contributing cause.

ROMANTIC NATURE

From classical antiquity through most of the eighteenth century the word nature had meant the sum total of existence, the entire cosmos and its laws and activity. When the so-called cult of nature arose in the Romantic Movement, the term had already come to mean something more limited in its connotations: the world apart from man's achievements, the landscape and countryside, the sea and the mountains. . . .

The Romantics moved out from the boudoir and salon to the field and hillside, just as for them the delights of social interchange were supplanted by private reverie, melancholy introspection, and the contemplation of the overflowing heart. Doubts about progress, civilization, and the primacy of intellect were augmented when it seemed likely that men were better in a state of nature. Perhaps the noble savage, the child, the simple uneducated rustic still partook of the Golden Age when mankind had hearts rather than purses of gold; when there were no *mine* and *thine,* no artificial laws, no hierarchy among persons. In vain did rigorous minds fight a rearguard action, and Voltaire — speaking of Rousseau — refuse to go down on all fours to become an infant once again. Humanitarian and democratic tendencies were too powerful. When the franchise was finally extended to the poor and humble, it was partly because they were felt to inculcate values that were not possessed by those of intellect or social rank.

Those "presences of nature" about which Wordsworth rhapsodized had still more cogency for certain select and dedicated souls. The eighteenth-century philosophers had made much of natural theology as opposed to revealed theology; that is, they held that the presence of God in the universe could be proved by an examination of the structure of the world. Since the world appeared to act in accordance with general scientific laws, and laws are created by intellects, reasoning by analogy would lead to establishing an Intelligence who made the cosmos and has continued to stand behind its operations. This was quite in keeping with deistic tenets. Pantheism, the philosophic attitude of so many Romantics, approached the problem very differently. . . . As one might expect, generations convinced of the primacy of intuitive thinking, of the eyes of the soul seeing farther and deeper than the eyes of the mind, found the analytical method of rationalism uncongenial or at best severely limited. Hence Wordsworth feels a "sense sublime" behind external phenomena. Not only were nature and mind exquisitely fitted, but they were parts of a Mighty Mind, the Oversoul of Emerson, an immanent God manifested through all forms of nature. Those initiates who, like Pope's "poor Indian," could see God in the clouds, required no superior intellectual powers for their sacred task; indeed, the meddling intellect impeded the possibility of true vision. Such notions of the pantheists indicated a reversion to a special and very private mysticism; and it is no wonder that institutionalized religions condemned their doctrine, or that the older Wordsworth deprecated his own youthful pantheistic exuberance when he became a pillar of the Church of England. It is interesting too that this way of looking at life found more enthusiastic adherents in northern Protestant countries such as Germany and England than in Catholic France or Italy. . . .

THE ROMANTIC REVOLUTIONS

. . . Previous ages had made no special demands on the intellectual or the artist to take a definite political stand. Men of letters often fought for causes — Dante for the White Guelfs in fourteenth-century Italy, Cervantes against the Turks at Lepanto — or they became political pamphleteers, like many of the English Augustans. But there seemed to be no necessary connection between two spheres of activity, the active and the contemplative. From 1789 through 1848, the social upheavals posed a problem that is still with us. At a time when certain critics pointed to a *necessary* relation between art and society, and Heine condemned the art of certain German Romantics for being Catholic and politically reactionary, the role of the artist-intellectual became more complicated. He was faced with a conflict between art for art's sake and art for the sake of society. If he chose the first, the artist stayed *au dessus de la mêlée,* as the embodiment of Thomas Mann's Unpolitical Man. . . . Yet this fine detachment seemed increasingly difficult to maintain in a world where the man of letters depended on a new literate, middle-class audience. With the disappearance of the patronage system in the Renaissance and the eighteenth century, there also passed away the small aristocratic, cultivated audiences that were a guarantee to the writer's own taste. On this issue the

Romantics split, and the fissure has never been repaired. . . .

THE ROMANTIC ARTIST

The Romantic movement was the last time that artists threw down the gauntlet to society and challenged their opponents to open warfare. The fight is not over, but then perhaps Romanticism is not entirely dead either. The superiority of intuitive over ratiocinative processes in the psyche meant that the imagination, like the mysterious phenomenon of love, was exalted to a position it had rarely enjoyed in the past. . . .

. . . By the end of the eighteenth century a new type of artist began slowly to emerge, and ordinary men found him puzzling. Goethe's play *Torquato Tasso* (1789) is one of the first delineations of the creative individual who feels himself a marked man. Genius is his, as well as the respect of his benefactors; and gladly they bestow the laurel crown upon his brow. But he feels an apartness from them that they cannot be expected to understand. The play ends with his nervous outburst. He leaves the Renaissance court where he has tried to find happiness, and we are left with the hope that eventual maturity will provide an adjustment. Here is the basic theme, and the real and fictional lives of subsequent Romantic artists were counterpoints over this *cantus firmus*. . . . Add to this burden the conviction that the artist was a guide to society, but that society often scorned its saviors; add the increasing difficulties of physical existence in a workaday, middle-class world where only "practical" activity is rewarded — and you have the artist's problem. Like so much of Romanticism, it is still with us.

The Need to Distinguish Romanticisms

ARTHUR O. LOVEJOY

In the first of the following selections, Arthur O. Lovejoy (1873–1962), long a professor of philosophy at Johns Hopkins University and one of the founders of the discipline of the history of ideas in America, outlines a program to overcome the confusion which results from the loose usage of the term, Romanticism. This essay, as the recurrent reference to it in other selections in this volume will indicate, has served as a center of controversy since its publication in 1924. Other essays in his *Essays in the History of Ideas*, and his classic *The Great Chain of Being*, trace the affinities of idea complexes in accordance with the program he outlined. The second selection is from *The Great Chain of Being*. Here we find Lovejoy's nearest approach to a comprehensive definition of Romanticism, as well as a concluding characteristically balanced evaluation of the effects of Romanticism.

ON THE DISCRIMINATION OF ROMANTICISMS

IT was apparently in 1824 that those respected citizens of La-Ferté-sous-Jouarre, MM. Dupuis and Cotonet, began an enterprise which was to cause them, as is recorded, "twelve years of suffering," and to end in disillusionment — the enterprise of discovering what Romanticism is, by collecting definitions and characterizations of it given by eminent authorities; . . . the contemporary collector of such articles, while paying tribute to the assiduity and the sufferings of those worthy pioneers of a century ago, will chiefly feel an envious sense of the relative simplicity of their task. He will find, also, that the apparent incongruity of the senses in which the term is employed has fairly kept pace with their increase in number; and that the singular potency which the subject has from the first possessed to excite controversy and breed divisions has in no degree diminished with the lapse of years.

For if some Dupuis of to-day were to gather, first, merely a few of the more recent accounts of the origin and age of Romanticism, he would learn from M. Lasserre and many others that Rousseau was the father of it; from Mr. Russell and Mr. Santayana that the honor of paternity might plausibly be claimed by Immanuel Kant; from M. Seillière that its grandparents were Fénelon and Madame Guyon; from Professor Babbitt that its earliest well-identified forebear was Francis Bacon; from Mr. Gosse that it originated in the bosom of the Reverend Joseph Warton; from the late Professor Ker that it had "its beginnings in the seventeenth-century" or a little earlier, in such books as "the *Arcadia* or the *Grand Cyrus*"; from Mr. J. E. G. de Montmorency that it "was born in the eleventh century, and sprang from that sense of aspiration which runs through the Anglo-French, or rather, the Anglo-Norman Renaissance"; from Professor Grierson that St. Paul's "irruption into Greek religious thought and Greek prose" was an essential example of "a romantic movement," though the "first great romantic" was Plato; and from Mr. Charles Whibley that the Odys-

From *Essays in the History of Ideas,* by Arthur O. Lovejoy, pp. 228–237, copyright 1948 by The Johns Hopkins Press.

sey is romantic in its "very texture and essence," but that, with its rival, Romanticism was "born in the Garden of Eden" and that, "the Serpent was the first romantic." The inquirer would, at the same time, find that many of these originators of Romanticism — including both the first and last mentioned, whom, indeed, some contemporaries are unable to distinguish — figure on other lists as initiators or representatives of tendencies of precisely the contrary sort.

These differing versions of the age and lineage of Romanticism are matched by a corresponding diversity in the descriptions offered by those of our time who have given special care to the observation of it. For Professor Ker Romanticism was "the fairy way of writing," and for Mr. Gosse it is inconsistent with "keeping to the facts"; but for Mr. F. Y. Eccles (following M. Pellissier) "the romantic system of ideas" is the direct source of "the realistic error," of the tendency to conceive of psychology as "the dry notation of purely physiological phenomena" and consequently to reduce the novel and the drama to the description of "the automaton-like gestures of *la bête humaine.*" To Professor Ker, again, "romantic" implies "reminiscence": "the romantic schools have always depended more or less on the past." Similarly Mr. Geoffrey Scott finds "its most typical form" to be "the cult of the extinct." But Professor Schelling tells us that "the classic temper studies the past, the romantic temper neglects it; . . . it leads us forward and creates new precedents"; while for some of the French "Romantic" critics of the 1820s and 1830s, the slogan of the movement was *il faut être de son temps.* . . . Among those for whom the word implies, *inter alia,* a social and political ideology and temper, one writer, typical of many, tells us that "Romanticism spells anarchy in every domain . . . a systematic hostility to everyone invested with any particle of social authority — husband or *pater-familias,* policeman or magistrate, priest or Cabinet minister"; but Professor Goetz Briefs finds "the climax of political

and economic thought within the Romantic movement" in the doctrine of Adam Müller, which sought to vindicate the sanctity of established social authority embodied in the family and the state; "by an inescapable logic the Romanticist ideology was drawn into the camp of reaction." . . . The function of the human mind which is to be regarded as peculiarly "romantic" is for some "the heart as opposed to the head," for others, "the Imagination, as contrasted with Reason and the Sense of Fact" — which I take to be ways of expressing a by no means synonymous pair of psychological antitheses. Typical manifestations of the spiritual essense of Romanticism have been variously conceived to be a passion for moonlight, for red waistcoats, for Gothic churches, for futurist paintings; for talking exclusively about oneself, for hero-worship, for losing oneself in an ecstatic contemplation of nature.

The offspring with which Romanticism is credited are as strangely assorted as its attributes and its ancestors. It is by different historians — sometimes by the same historians — supposed to have begotten the French Revolution and the Oxford Movement; the Return to Rome and the Return to the State of Nature; the philosophy of Hegel, the philosophy of Schopenhauer, and the philosophy of Nietzsche — than which few other three philosophies more nearly exhaust the rich possibilities of philosophic disagreement; the revival of neo-Platonic mysticism in a Coleridge or an Alcott, the Emersonian transcendentalism, and scientific materialism; Wordsworth and Wilde; Newman and Huxley; the Waverly novels, the *Comédie Humaine,* and *Les Rougon-Macquart.* M. Seillière and Professor Babbitt have been especially active in tracing the progeny of Romanticism in the past century; the extraordinary number and still more extraordinary diversity of the descendants of it discovered by their researches are known to all here, and it therefore suffices to refer to their works for further examples. . . .

The result is a confusion of terms, and

of ideas, beside which that of a hundred years ago — mind-shaking though it was to the honest inquirers of La-Ferté-sous-Jouarre — seems pure lucidity. The word "romantic" has come to mean so many things that, by itself, it means nothing. It has ceased to perform the function of a verbal sign. When a man is asked, as I have had the honor of being asked to discuss Romanticism, it is impossible to know what ideas or tendencies he is to talk about, when they are supposed to have flourished, or in whom they are supposed to be chiefly exemplified. Perhaps there are some who think the rich ambiguity of the word not regrettable. . . . But for one of the philosopher's trade, at least, the situation is embarrassing and exasperating; for philosophers, in spite of a popular belief to the contrary, are persons who suffer from a morbid solicitude to know what they are talking about.

Least of all does it seem possible, while the present uncertainty concerning the nature and locus of Romanticism prevails, to take sides in the controversy which still goes on so briskly with respect to its merits, the character of its general influence upon art and life. To do so would be too much like consenting to sit on a jury to try a criminal not yet identified, for a series of apparently incompatible crimes, before a bench of learned judges engaged in accusing one another of being accessories to whatever mischief has been done. It is to be observed, for example, that Messrs. Lasserre, Seillière, Babbitt and More (to mention no others) are engaged in arguing that something called Romanticism is the chief cause of the spiritual evils from which the nineteenth century and our own have suffered; but that they represent at least three different opinions as to what these evils are and how they are to be remedied. M. Lasserre, identifying Romanticism with the essential spirit of the French Revolution, finds the chief cause of our woes in that movement's breach with the past, in its discarding of the ancient traditions of European civilization; and he consequently seeks the cure in a return to an older faith and an older political and social order, and in an abandonment of the optimistic fatalism generated by the idea of progress. M. Seillière, however, holds that "the spirit of the Revolution in that in which it is rational, Stoic, Cartesian, classical . . . is justified, enduring, assured of making its way in the world more and more"; and that, consequently, the ill name of Romanticism should be applied to the revolutionary movement only where it has deviated from its true course, in "the social mysticism, the communistic socialism of the present time." He therefore intimates that the school of opinion which M. Lasserre ably represents is itself a variety of Romanticism. . . .

What, then, can be done to clear up, or to diminish, this confusion of terminology and of thought which has for a century been the scandal of literary history and criticism, and is still, as it would not be difficult to show, copiously productive of historical errors and of dangerously undiscriminating diagnoses of the moral and aesthetic maladies of our age? The one really radical remedy — namely, that we should all cease talking about Romanticism — is, I fear, certain not to be adopted. It would probably be equally futile to attempt to prevail upon scholars and critics to restrict their use of the term to a single and reasonably well-defined sense. Such a proposal would only be the starting-point of a new controversy. Men, and especially philologists, will doubtless go on using words as they like, however much annoyance they cause philosophers by this unchartered freedom. There are, however, two possible historical inquiries which, if carried out more thoroughly and carefully than has yet been done, would, I think, do much to rectify the present muddle, and would at the same time promote a clearer understanding of the general movement of ideas, the logical and psychological relations between the chief episodes and transitions, in modern thought and taste.

One of these measures would be somewhat analogous to the procedure of contemporary psychopathologists in the treatment of certain types of disorder. It has, we are told, been found that some mental disturbances can be cured or alleviated by making the patient explicitly aware of the genesis of his troublesome "complex," i.e., by enabling him to reconstruct those processes of association of ideas through which it was formed. Similarly in the present case, I think, it would be useful to trace the associative processes through which the word "romantic" has attained its present amazing diversity, and consequent uncertainty, of connotation and denotation; in other words, to carry out an adequate semasiological study of the term. For one of the few things certain about Romanticism is that the name of it offers one of the most complicated, fascinating, and instructive of all problems in semantics. It is, in short, a part of the task of the historian of ideas, when he applies himself to the study of the thing or things called Romanticism, to render it, if possible, psychologically intelligible how such manifold and discrepant phenomena have all come to receive one name. Such an analysis would, I am convinced, show us a large mass of purely verbal confusions operative as actual factors in the movement of thought in the past century and a quarter; and it would, by making these confusions explicit, make it easier to avoid them.

But this inquiry would in practice, for the most part, be inseparable from a second, which is the remedy that I wish, on this occasion, especially to recommend. The first step in this second mode of treatment of the disorder is that we should learn to use the word "Romanticism" in the plural. This, of course, is already the practice of the more cautious and observant literary historians, in so far as they recognize that the "Romanticism" of one country may have little in common with that of another, and at all events ought to be defined in distinctive terms. But the discrimination of the Romanticisms which I have in mind is not solely or chiefly a division upon lines of nationality or language. What is needed is that any study of the subject should begin with a recognition of a *prima-facie* plurality of Romanticisms, of possibly quite distinct thought-complexes, a number of which may appear in one country. There is no hope of clear thinking on the part of the student of modern literature, if — as alas! has been repeatedly done by eminent writers — he vaguely hypostatizes the term, and starts with the presumption that "Romanticism" is the heaven-appointed designation of some single real entity, or type of entities, to be found in nature. He must set out from the simple and obvious fact that there are various historic episodes or movements to which different historians of our own or other periods have, for one reason or another, given the name. There is a movement which began in Germany in the seventeen-nineties — the only one which has an indisputable title to be called Romanticism, since it invented the term for its own use. There is another movement which began pretty definitely in England in the seventeen-forties. There is a movement which began in France in 1801. There is another movement which began in France in the second decade of the century, is linked with the German movement, and took over the German name. There is the rich and incongruous collection of ideas to be found in Rousseau. There are numerous other things called Romanticism by various writers whom I cited at the outset. The fact that the same name has been given by different scholars to all of these episodes is no evidence, and scarcely even establishes a presumption, that they are identical in essentials. There may be some common denominator of them all; but if so, it has never yet been clearly exhibited, and its presence is not to be assumed *a priori*. In any case, each of these so-called Romanticisms was a highly complex and usually an exceedingly unstable intellectual compound; each, in other words, was made up of various unit-ideas linked together, for the most part, not by any indissoluble bonds of logical necessity, but by alogical associative processes, greatly facilitated and partly caused, in the case of the Romanticisms which grew up after the appellation "Romantic" was invented, by the congenital and acquired ambiguities of the word. And when certain of these Romanticisms have in truth significant elements in common, they are not necessarily the same elements in any two cases. Romanticism A may have one characteristic presupposition or impulse, X, which it shares with Romanticism B, another characteristic, Y, which it shares with Romanticism C, to which X is wholly foreign. In the case, moreover, of those movements or schools to which the label was applied in their own time, the contents under the label sometimes changed radically and rapidly. At the end of a decade or two you had the same men and the same party appellation, but profoundly different ideas. As everyone knows, this is precisely what happened in the case of what is called French Romanticism. It may or may not be true that, as M. A. Viatte has sought to show, at the beginning of this process of transformation some subtle leaven was already at work which made the final outcome inevitable; the fact remains that in most of its practically significant sympathies and affiliations of a literary, ethical, political, and religious sort, the French "Romanticism" of the eighteen-thirties was the antithesis of that of the beginning of the century.

But the essential of the second remedy is that each of these Romanticisms — after they are first thus roughly discriminated with respect to their representatives or their dates — should be resolved, by a more thorough and discerning analysis than is yet customary, into its elements — into the several ideas and aesthetic susceptibilities of which it is composed. Only after these fundamental thought-factors or emotive strains in it are clearly discriminated and fairly exhaustively enumerated, shall we be in a position to judge of the degree of its affinity with other complexes to which the same name has been applied, to see precisely what tacit preconceptions or controlling motives or explicit contentions were common to any two or more of them, and wherein they manifested distinct and divergent tendencies.

ROMANTICISM AND PLENITUDE

. . . The Enlightenment was, in short, an age devoted, at least in its dominant tendency, to the simplification and the standardization of thought and life — to their standardization by means of their simplification. Spinoza summed it up in a remark reported by one of his early biographers: "The purpose of Nature is to make men uniform, as children of a common mother." The struggle to realize this supposed purpose of nature, the general attack upon the *differentness* of men and their opinions and valuations and institutions — this, with the resistances to it and the eventual revulsion against it, was the central and dominating fact in the intellectual history of Europe from the late sixteenth to the late eighteenth century.

There have, in the entire history of thought, been few changes in standards of value more profound and more momentous than that which took place when the contrary principle began widely to prevail — when it came to be believed not only that in many, or in all, phases of human life there are diverse excellences, but that diversity itself is of the essence of excellence; and that of art, in particular, the objective is neither the attainment of some single ideal perfection of form in a small number

Reprinted by permission of the publishers from Arthur O. Lovejoy's *The Great Chain of Being*, Cambridge, Mass.: Harvard University Press. Copyright 1936, 1964 by the President and Fellows of Harvard College, pp. 292–294, 298–299, 303–307, 311–313.

of fixed *genres* nor the gratification of that least common denominator of aesthetic susceptibility which is shared by all mankind in all ages, but rather the fullest possible expression of the abundance of different-ness that there is, actually or potentially, in nature and human nature, and — for the function of the artist in relation to his public — the evocation of capacities for understanding, sympathy, enjoyment, which are as yet latent in most men, and perhaps never capable of universalization. And these assumptions, though assuredly not the only important, are the one *common*, factor in a number of otherwise diverse tendencies which, by one or another critic or historian, have been termed "Romantic": the immense multiplication of genres and of verse-forms; the admission of the aesthetic legitimacy of the *genre mixte*; the *goût de la nuance*; the naturalization in art of the "grotesque"; the quest for local color; the endeavor to reconstruct in imagination the distinctive inner life of peoples remote in time or space or in cultural condition; the *étalage du moi*; the demand for particularized fidelity in landscape-description; the revulsion against simplicity; the distrust of universal formulas in politics; the aesthetic antipathy to standardization; the identification of the Absolute with the "concrete universal' in metaphysics; the feeling of "the glory of the imperfect"; the cultivation of individual, national, and racial peculiarities; the depreciation of the obvious and the general high valuation (wholly foreign to most earlier periods) of originality, and the usually futile and absurd self-conscious pursuit of that attribute. It is, however, of no great consequence whether or not we apply to this transformation of current assumptions about value the name of "Romanticism"; what it is essential to remember is that the transformation has taken place and that it, perhaps, more than any other *one* thing has distinguished, both for better and worse, the prevailing assumptions of the mind of the nineteenth and of our own century from those of the preceding period in the intellectual history

of the West. That change, in short, has consisted in the substitution of what may be called diversitarianism for uniformitarianism as the ruling preconception in most of the normative provinces of thought. . . .

. . . It remains the fact that, throughout the Enlightenment, the uniformitarian creed *had* in practice been effectively dominant — while the theoretical premises of diversitarianism had, in the same period, been constantly and with increasing frequency dilated upon, and that their practical implications did eventually find acceptance and application. It also, I think, remains the fact that, even though it be assumed — as I am not prepared to assume without a good deal of qualification — that the reasons which men give for their beliefs, their standards, and their tastes are but the "rationalization" of their desires and their spontaneous likings and dislikes, the possibility of giving reasons, or what appear to be such, is not less indispensable. And it was in the principle of plenitude that the protagonists of the revolution with which we are here concerned found one of the two most fundamental and, for their generation, most effective of their reasons. . . .

In the writings (after 1796) of the German poets, critics, and moralists who adapted the word "romantic" to their own uses and introduced it into the vocabulary of literary history and of philosophy, the diversitarian assumption is pervasively present; and here too it is closely connected with the conception that the artist's task is to imitate, not simply Nature's works, but her way of working, to enter into the spirit of the universe by aiming, as it does, at fullness and variety without end. . . .

But there was a radical and perilous ambiguity in this assumption when it was applied as a rule of art or of conduct. It could be construed in two ways; and they tended in practice to be antithetic ways, though they were not wholly so in essence. On the one hand, it suggested, as both an aesthetic and a moral aim for the individual, the effort to enter as fully as possible into the immensely various range of thought and feeling in other men. It thus made for the cultivation, not merely of tolerance, but of imaginative insight into the points of view, the valuations, the tastes, the subjective experiences, of others; and this not only as a means to the enrichment of one's own inner life, but also as a recognition of the objective validity of diversities of valuation. . . . The earlier Romantic writers accordingly became zealous preachers of catholicity in aesthetic appreciation. . . .

For the artist, as distinct from the appreciator of art, this ideal led to the program expressed in Friedrich Schlegel's famous definition of Romantic poetry: "die romantische Poesie ist eine progressive Universalpoesie" [romantic poetry is a progressive universal poetry]. It must be universal, not in the restrictive sense of seeking uniformity of norms and universality of appeal, but in the expansive sense of aiming at the apprehension and expression of every mode of human experience. Nothing should be too strange or too remote, nothing too lofty or too low, to be included in its scope; no *nuance* of character or emotion can be so delicate and elusive, or so peculiar, that the poet or novelist ought not to attempt to seize it and to convey its unique *quale* to his readers. "From the romantic point of view," wrote Schlegel, "the abnormal species (*Abarten*) of literature also have their value — even the eccentric and monstrous — as materials and preparatory exercises for universality — provided only that there is *something* in them, that they are really original." . . .

But the idealization of diversity, the program of consciously emulating and even adding to the plenitude of nature, could, as I have said, be quite otherwise interpreted. And this alternative interpretation is apparent in the same group of writers, and even in the same individuals. If the world is the better the more variety it contains, the more adequately it manifests the possibilities of differentness in human nature, the duty of the individual, it would seem, was to cherish and intensify his own

differentness from other men. Diversitarianism thus led also to a conscious pursuit of idiosyncrasy, personal, racial, national, and, so to say, chronological. "It is precisely individuality," wrote Friedrich Schlegel in the *Athenaeum,* "that is the original and eternal thing in men. . . . The cultivation and development of this individuality, as one's highest vocation, would be a divine egoism." "The more personal, local, peculiar (*eigentümlicher*), of its own time (*temporeller*), a poem is, the nearer it stands to the centre of poetry," declared Novalis. This, obviously, was the polar opposite of the fundamental principle of the neo-classic aesthetic doctrine. This interpretation of the Romantic ideal suggested that the first and great commandment is: "Be yourself, which is to say, be unique!" . . .

If we should attempt, in the light of subsequent history, an appraisal of these two strains in the Romantic ideal most of us would perhaps agree that both contributed to bring about some happy and some unhappy consequences in the next dozen decades. The first strain was the promulgation and the prophecy of an immense increase in the range — though not always in the excellence — of most of the arts, and of an unprecedented widening of men's gusto in the recognition and the enjoyment of what Akenside had called "the fair variety of things." The program of the early Romantic school *was* to be the deliberate program of the drama, much of the non-dramatic poetry, the novel, music, and painting in the nineteenth century; and it is mere blindness not to see in this a vast enrichment of the sources of delight in life. And this was not merely an aesthetic gain. It tended — in so far as it was not offset by an opposing tendency — to nothing less than an enlargement of human nature itself — to an increase of men's, and nations', understanding and appreciation of one another, not as a multitude of samples of an identical model, but as representatives of a legitimate and welcome diversity of cultures and of individual reactions to the world which we have in common. Yet all this had its dangers. . . . The revolt against the standardization of life easily becomes a revolt against the whole conception of standards. The God whose attribute of reasonableness was expressed in the principle of plenitude was not selective; he gave reality to all the essences. But there is in man a reason which demands selection, preference, and negation, in conduct and in art. To say "Yes" to everything and everybody is manifestly to have no character at all. The delicate and difficult art of life is to find, in each new turn of experience, the *via media* between two extremes: to be catholic *without* being characterless; to have and apply standards, and yet to be on guard against their desensitizing and stupefying influence, their tendency to blind us to the diversities of concrete situations and to previously unrecognized values; to know when to tolerate, when to embrace, and when to fight. And in that art, since no fixed and comprehensive rule can be laid down for it, we shall doubtless never attain perfection. All this has now, no doubt, become a truism; but it is also a paradox, since it demands a synthesis of opposites. And to Schiller and some of the Romanticists its paradoxical aspect made it seem not less but more evidently true.

A similar bifurcation of tendencies may be seen in the other of the two elements in the Romantic ideal, as an influence in the subsequent century. It served to promote, in individuals and in peoples, a resistance to those forces, resultant largely from the spread of democracy and from technological progress, which tend to obliterate the differences that make men, and groups of men, interesting and therefore valuable to one another. It was the perpetual enemy of *das Gemeine*. But it has also (being in

this precisely opposite to the other Romantic tendency) promoted a great deal of sickly and sterile introversion in literature — a tiresome exhibition of the eccentricities of the individual Ego, these eccentricities being often, as is now notorious, merely conventions painfully turned inside out, since a man cannot by taking thought become more original or "unique" than Nature has made him. It has lent itself all too easily to the service of man's egotism, and especially — in the political and social sphere — of the kind of collective vanity which is nationalism or racialism. The belief in the sanctity of one's idiosyncrasy — especially if it be a group idiosyncrasy, and therefore sustained and intensified by mutual flattery — is rapidly converted into a belief in its superiority. More than one great people, in the course of the past century and a half, having first made a god of its own peculiarities, good or bad or both, presently began to suspect that there was no other god. A type of national culture valued at first because it was one's own, and because the conservation of differentness was recognized as a good for humanity as a whole, came in time to be conceived of as a thing which one had a mission to impose upon others, or to diffuse over as large a part of the surface of the planet as possible. Thus the wheel came full circle; what may be called a particularistic uniformitarianism, a tendency to seek to universalize things originally valued because they were not universal, found expression in poetry, in a sort of philosophy, in the policies of great states and the enthusiasms of their populations. The tragic outcome has been seen, and experienced, by all of us in our own time. . . .

The Unity of the Romantic Movement

RENÉ WELLEK

René Wellek is professor of Comparative Literature at Yale University. He is widely known as a critic, aesthetic theorist (e.g. in his and Austin Warren's *Theory of Literature*), and as a literary historian. His major work in the latter field is his monumental *A History of Modern Criticism, 1750–1950*. In the following selection he confronts Lovejoy's hesitation to set up a firm definition of romanticism — what he calls Lovejoy's "nominalism" — with what he considers the "common denominator" of the distinct national romanticisms. He traces the "relative differences" of these several romanticisms to social and historical causes.

I. THE TERM "ROMANTIC" AND ITS DERIVATIVES

The terms "romanticism" and "romantic" have been under attack for a long time. In a well-known paper, "On the Discriminations of Romanticisms," Arthur O. Lovejoy has argued impressively that "the word 'romantic' has come to mean so many things that, by itself, it means nothing. It has ceased to perform the function of a verbal sign." Lovejoy proposed to remedy this "scandal of literary history and criticism" by showing that "the 'Romanticism' of one country may have little in common with that of another, that there is, in fact, a plurality of Romanticisms, of possibly quite distinct thought-complexes." He grants that "there may be some common denominator to them all; but if so, it has never been clearly exhibited." Moreover, according to Lovejoy, "the romantic ideas were in large part heterogeneous, logically independent, and sometimes essentially antithetic to one another in their implications."

As far as I know, this challenge has never been taken up by those who still consider the terms useful and will continue to speak of a unified European romantic movement. While Lovejoy makes reservations and some concessions to the older view, the impression seems widespread today, especially among American scholars, that his thesis has been established securely. I propose to show that there is no basis for this extreme nominalism, that the major romantic movements form a unity of theories, philosophies, and style, and that these, in turn, form a coherent group of ideas each of which implicates the other.

I have tried elsewhere to make a theoretical defense of the use and function of period terms. I concluded that one must conceive of them, not as arbitrary linguistic labels nor as metaphysical entities, but as names for systems of norms which dominate literature at a specific time of the historical process. The term "norms" is a convenient term for conventions, themes, philosophies, styles, and the like, while the word "domination" means the prevalence of one set of norms compared with the prevalence of another set in the past. The term "domination" must not be conceived of statistically: it is entirely possible to envisage a situation in which older norms still prevailed numerically while the new conventions were created or used by writers of greatest artistic importance. It thus seems

From "The Concept of 'Romanticism' in Literary History," *Comparative Literature*, vol. I, no. 1, 1949, pp. 1–3, 16–17, 19–20, 23; vol. I, no. 2, 1949, pp. 147–156, 158–159, 161, 165–172. By permission of *Comparative Literature* and the author.

to me impossible to avoid the critical problem of evaluation in literary history. . . .

In the case of romanticism the question of the terminology, its spread and establishment, is especially complicated because it is contemporary or nearly contemporary with the phenomena described. The adoption of the terms points to an awareness of certain changes. But this awareness may have existed without these terms, or these terms may have been introduced before the actual changes took place, merely as a program, as the expression of a wish, an incitement to change. The situation differs in different countries; but this is, of course, in itself no argument that the phenomena to which the terms refer showed substantial differences.

The semantic history of the term "romantic" has been very fully studied in its early stages in France, England, and Germany, and for the later stages in Germany. But, unfortunately, little attention has been paid to it in other countries and, even where materials are abundant, it is still difficult to ascertain when, for the first time, a work of literature and which works of literature were designated as "romantic," when the contrast of "classical-romantic" was introduced, when a contemporary writer referred to himself first as a "romanticist," when the term "romanticism" was first adopted in a country, etc. . . .

If we survey the evidence assembled we can hardly escape several conclusions which seem important for our argument. The self-designation of writers and poets as "romantic" varies in the different countries considerably; many examples are late and of short duration. If we take self-designation as the basic criterion for modern use, there would be no romantic movement in Germany before 1808, none in France before 1818 or (since the 1818 example was an isolated instance, Stendhal) before 1824, and none at all in England. If we take the use of the word "romantic" for any kind of literature (at first mediæval romances, Tasso, and Ariosto) as our criterion, we are thrown back to 1669 in France, 1673 in England, 1698 in Germany. If we insist on taking the contrast between the terms "classical and romantic" as decisive, we arrive at the dates 1801 for Germany, 1810 for France, 1811 for England, 1816 for Italy, etc. If we think that a realization of the quality of romanticism is particularly important, we would find the term "Romantik" in Germany in 1802, "Romantisme" in France in 1816, "Romanticismo" in Italy in 1818, and "Romanticism" in England in 1823. Surely, all these facts (even though the dates may be corrected) point to the conclusion that the history of the term and its introduction cannot regulate the usage of the modern historian, since he would be forced to recognize milestones in his history which are not justified by the actual state of the literatures in question. The great changes happened, independently of the introduction of these terms either before or after them and only rarely approximately at the same time.

On the other hand, the usual conclusion drawn from examinations of the history of the words, that they are used in contradictory senses, seems to me greatly exaggerated. One must grant that many German æstheticians juggle the terms in extravagant and personal ways, nor can one deny that the emphasis on different aspects of their meaning shifts from writer to writer and sometimes from nation to nation. But, on the whole, there was really no misunderstanding about the meaning of "romanticism" as a new designation for poetry, opposed to the poetry of neoclassicism, and drawing its inspiration and models from the Middle Ages and the Renaissance. The term is understood in this sense all over Europe, and everywhere we find references to August Wilhelm Schlegel or Madame de Staël and their particular formulas opposing "classical" and "romantic."

The fact that the convenient terms were introduced sometimes much later than the time when actual repudiation of the neoclassical tradition was accomplished does not, of course, prove that the changes were not noticed at that time.

The mere use of the terms "romantic"

and "romanticism" must not be overrated. English writers early had a clear consciousness that there was a movement which rejected the critical concepts and poetic practice of the eighteenth century, that it formed a unity, and had its parallels on the continent, especially in Germany. Without the term "romantic" we can trace, within a short period, the shift from the earlier conception of the history of English poetry as one of a uniform progress from Waller and Denham to Dryden and Pope, still accepted in Johnson's *Lives of the Poets,* to Southey's opposite view in 1807, that the "time which elapsed from the days of Dryden to those of Pope is the dark age of English poetry." . . .

The most boldly formulated definition of the new view is again in Southey, in the "Sketches of the Progress of English Poetry from Chaucer to Cowper" (1833). There the "age from Dryden to Pope" is called "the worst age of English poetry: the age of Pope was the pinchbeck age of poetry." "If Pope closed the door against poetry, Cowper opened it." The same view, though less sharply expressed, can be found with increasing frequency even in textbooks, such as Robert Chambers' *History of the English Language and Literature* (1836), in De Quincey's writings, and R. H. Horne's *New Spirit of the Age* (1884).

None of these publications use the term "romantic," but in all of them we hear that there is a new age of poetry which has a new style inimical to that of Pope. The emphasis and selections of examples vary, but in combination they say that the German influence, the revival of the ballads and the Elizabethans, and the French Revolution were the decisive influences which brought about the change. Thomson, Burns, Cowper, Gray, Collins, and Chatterton are honored as precursors, Percy and the Wartons as initiators. The trio, Wordsworth, Coleridge and Southey, are recognized as the founders and, as time progressed, Byron, Shelley, and Keats are added in spite of the fact that this new

group of poets denounced the older for political reasons. . . .

This general scheme is, to my mind, still substantially valid. It seems an unwarranted nominalism to reject it completely and to speak, as Ronald S. Crane does, of "the fairy tales about neoclassicism and romanticism" in the eighteenth century. . . .

. . . We can, it seems, go on speaking of "pre-romanticism" and romanticism, since there are periods of the dominance of a system of ideas and poetic practices which have their anticipations in the preceding decades. The terms "romantic" and "romanticism," though late by the dates of their introduction, were everywhere understood in approximately the same sense and are still useful as terms for the kind of literature produced after neoclassicism.

In the second half of this paper I shall attempt to show that this body of literature forms a unity if we apply a few simple criteria and that the same criteria are valid for all the three major romantic movements — English, French, and German. . . .

II. THE UNITY OF EUROPEAN ROMANTICISM

If we examine the characteristics of the actual literature which called itself or was called "romantic" all over the continent, we find throughout Europe the same conceptions of poetry and of the workings and nature of poetic imagination, the same conception of nature and its relation to man, and basically the same poetic style, with a use of imagery, symbolism, and myth which is clearly distinct from that of eighteenth-century neoclassicism. This conclusion might be strengthened or modified by attention to other frequently discussed elements: subjectivism, mediævalism, folklore, etc. But the following three criteria should be particularly convincing, since each is central for one aspect of the practice of literature: imagination for the view of poetry, nature for the view of the world, and symbol and myth for poetic style.

German literature is the clearest case; in both so-called romantic schools we find a view of poetry as knowledge of the deepest reality, of nature as a living whole, and of poetry as primarily myth and symbolism. This would hardly need to be argued with anyone who had read only Novalis. But it is impossible to accept the common German view that romanticism is the creation of the Schlegels, Tieck, Novalis, and Wackenroder. If one looks at the history of German literature between the date of Klopstock's *Messiah* (1748) and the death of Goethe (1832), one can hardly deny the unity and coherence of the whole movement which, in European terms, would have to be called "romantic." . . .

One must, of course, grant distinctions between the different stages of the development. There was the "Storm and Stress" movement in the seventies which exactly parallels what today is elsewhere called "preromanticism." It was more radical and violent than anything corresponding in England or France, but it must be recognized as substantially the same movement, if we realize that the most important single influence was that of Rousseau and understand the extraordinary extent to which the ideas of Herder were prepared by the English and Scottish critics of the eighteenth century. . . .

There was, one must admit, a pronounced stage of Hellenism in the German movement; its roots are in Winckelmann, an ardent student of Shaftesbury, and this Hellenic enthusiasm early became extremely fervid in Germany. . . . Still, one need not speak of a "Tyranny of Greece over Germany." There was, after all, a comparable Hellenic enthusiasm in France and England. . . .

If this view that a large part of Hellenism is romantic is justified, it will be possible to minimize the excessive stress the Germans have traditionally put on the supposed conflict between the "classicism" and "romanticism." . . . Still, there is a fundamental unity in the whole of German literature from roughly the middle of the eighteenth century to the death of Goethe. It is an attempt to create a new art different from that of the French seventeenth cen-

tury; it is an attempt at a new philosophy which is neither orthodox Christianity nor the Enlightenment of the eighteenth century. This new view emphasizes the totality of man's forces, not reason alone, nor sentiment alone, but rather intuition, "intellectual intuition," imagination. It is a revival of Neoplatonism, a pantheism (whatever its concessions to orthodoxy), a monism which arrived at identification of God and the world, soul and body, subject and object. The propounders of these ideas were always conscious of the precariousness and difficulty of these views, which frequently appeared to them only as distant ideals; hence the "unending desire" of the German romantics, the stress on evolution, on art as a groping towards the ideal. Exoticism of many kinds is part of the reaction against the eighteenth century and its self-complacency; the suppressed forces of the soul seek their analogies and models in prehistory, in the Orient, in the Middle Ages, and finally in India, as well as in the unconscious and in dreams.

The German romantic writers are the contemporaries of the flowering of German music: of Beethoven, Schubert, Schumann, Weber, and others, many of whom used German poetry of the age as texts for their songs or, like Beethoven, as inspiration for their symphonies. The fact of this collaboration is significant but hardly sufficient to make it the distinguishing characteristic of all romanticism. Such an emphasis obscures the international character of the movement, since the collaboration with music was practically nonexistent in England and fairly late and slight in France. It points to the undeniable fact that romanticism in Germany was far more pervasive than in the other countries and that it affected all human endeavors — philosophy, politics, philology, history, science, and all the other arts — there much more thoroughly than elsewhere. But in this respect also the difference between Germany and the other countries is only relative. There was a romantic philosophy, philology, history, politics, and even science, not to speak of painting and music, in other countries, especially in France (Delacroix, Berlioz, Michelet, Cousin). The apparent isolation of Germany is exaggerated by German writers who see in romanticism a purely German style, and by antiromantics and recently by anti-Hitler propagandists who want to prove that all the ills of the last two centuries came from Germany. The only view which takes account of all factors holds that romanticism is a general movement in European thought and art and that it has native roots in every major country. Cultural revolutions of such profound significance are not accomplished by mere importations.

Romanticism was more completely victorious in Germany than elsewhere for very obvious historical reasons. The German Enlightenment was weak and of short duration. The Industrial Revolution was late in coming. There was no leading rationalistic bourgeoisie. Both the derivative, unoriginal Enlightenment and the peculiarly rigid religious orthodoxies seemed unsatisfactory. Thus social and intellectual causes opened the way for a literature which was created mostly by unattached intellectuals, tutors, army surgeons, salt-mine officials, court clerks, and the like, who revolted against both feudalism and middle-class ideals. German romanticism, more so than English and French, was the movement of an intelligentsia which had loosened its class ties and hence was particularly apt to create a literature remote from ordinary reality and social concerns. . . .

While it would be absurd to deny the special features of the German romantic age (we may pause to reflect that every age has its special features), almost all its views and techniques can be paralleled elsewhere. It is no denial of originality to see that the great German writers drew freely on foreign sources (Rousseau, English preromanticism) or on sources in the remote past, both foreign and native, which had been available to the other European nations: Neoplatonism, Giodano Bruno, Böhme, a reinterpreted Spinoza, Leibniz. The Ger-

mans, in turn, influenced other countries; but their influence, for obvious chronological reasons, comes too late to make them the only source of the turn towards the ideas and poetic myths usually called romantic. In England, Böhme was important for Blake, Schelling and August Wilhelm Schlegel for Coleridge, Bürger and Goethe for Scott (though hardly centrally so), Goethe and Jean Paul for Carlyle. But the German influence on Wordsworth, Shelley, Keats, and even Byron is negligible. In France, German influences came much later; A. W. Schlegel, we have shown, was very important for the introduction of the new critical terminology. German interests are strong in Nodier, in Gérard de Nerval, and in Quinet, who studied Herder and Creuzer. Some argument can be made for the importance of the German song (*Lied*) for the French romantic lyric; but certainly the central figures, Chateaubriand, Lamartine, Vigny, Hugo, Balzac, have few German affinities, and similarities must be explained by identical antecedents in England and an analogous literary and cultural situation.

As for France, our view is blurred by the official insistence on beginning the romantic movement with the triumph of Hernani (1830), a minor event in a later perspective, which obscures the fact that, outside of the drama or rather the Parisian official stage, a profound change had come over French literature many years before. . . .

This French preromantic movement received a temporary setback through the Revolution, which fostered classicism and rationalism, and by the Empire, which also had its official classicism. But among the *emigrés* romanticism flourished. Madame de Staël was the propagandist of the German romantics. Chateaubriand cannot be made out a classicist, whatever his interests in classical antiquity and his reservations against Shakespeare or against many of his contemporaries. *Le Génie de Christianisme* (1802) is a romantic poetics. If we apply our tests, it is obvious that Chateaubriand expounds an organic symbolic order of nature, that he is a mythologist and symbolist *par excellence*. But Madame de Staël and Chateaubriand were by no means alone in their time; even Chénier conceived the idea of a new mythic poetry, especially in the fragment *Hermès*. In Sénancour's *Obermann* (1804) we find the romantic view of nature in full bloom. . . .

Victor Hugo, later in his life, became the most ambitious mythologist, symbolist, prophet of a new religion, of all the romantics. . . . In Hugo, then, all the romantic convictions and themes are summarized: organic, evolving nature, the view of poetry as prophecy, the view that symbol and myth are the instruments of poetry. In Hugo the reconciliation of opposites, the stress on the grotesque and evil ultimately absorbed in the harmony of the universe, is particularly clear and was clear even in his early aesthetic theories, as in the preface to *Cromwell*. His prophetic fervor, intensity, and grandiose gestures may have become pretentious and absurd to generations who have lost this view of poetry. But Hugo marshalled all the possible arguments for the romantic view of nature, for man's continuity with nature, the great scale of nature, and the final perfection of man. . . .

I have already suggested some of the sources of French romanticism — Swedenborg, St. Martin, the Germans. But we must realize that in all phases of French thought there was a considerable parallel activity. In history Michelet propounded a "historical symbolism." The numerous neo-Catholic French thinkers shared many of the main romantic tenets and motifs. There is "striking similarity between the doctrines of Hegel and Bonald." Joseph de Maistre, in his youth at least, was steeped in the mythical, Masonic, and Illuminati ideas of the time, and they left strong traces on his mature thought. . . .

The whole eclectic movement, fed as it is in part from German sources, especially Schelling, fits into our scheme, and much in the French science of the time, particu-larly biology, helps to re-create the whole mental "climate" in which French romanticism flourished.

Turning to England, we can see a complete agreement with the French and the Germans on all essential points. The great poets of the English romantic movement constitute a fairly coherent group, with the same view of poetry and the same conception of imagination, the same view of nature and mind. They share also a poetic style, a use of imagery, symbolism, and myth, which is quite distinct from anything that had been practiced by the eighteenth century, and which was felt by their contemporaries to be obscure and almost unintelligible.

The affinity of the concepts of imagination among the English romantic poets scarcely needs demonstration. . . . Thus imagination is not merely the power of visualization, somewhere in between sense and reason, which it had been to Aristotle or Addison, nor even the inventive power of the poet, which by Hume and many other eighteenth-century theorists was conceived of as a "combination of innate sensibility, the power of association, and the faculty of conception," but a creative power by which the mind "gains insight into reality, reads nature as a symbol of something behind or within nature not ordinarily perceived." Thus imagination is the basis of Blake's rejection of the mechanistic world picture, the basis of an idealistic epistemology —

The Sun's Light, when he unfolds it
Depends on the Organ that beholds it;

and, of course, the basis of an aesthetics, the justification of art and his own peculiar kind of art. This conception of imagination sufficiently justifies the necessity of myth and of metaphor and symbol as its vehicle. . . .

. . . Clarence D. Thorpe, in analyzing all of Keats relevant scattered pronouncements, concludes: "Such is the power of creative imagination, a seeing, reconciling, combining force that seizes the old, penetrates beneath its surface, disengages the truth slumbering there, and, building afresh, bodies forth anew a reconstructed universe in fair forms of artistic power and beauty." This could be a summary of the theories of imagination of all the romantic poets.

Clearly, such a theory implies a theory of reality and, especially, of nature. There are individual differences among the great romantic poets concerning the conception of nature. But all of them share a common objection to the mechanistic universe of the eighteenth century — even though Wordsworth admires Newton and accepts him, at least in the orthodox interpretation. All romantic poets conceived of nature as an organic whole, on the analogue of man rather than a concourse of atoms — a nature that is not divided from aesthetic values, which are just as real (or rather more real) than the abstractions of science. . . .

This conception of the nature of poetic imagination and of the universe has obvious consequences for poetic practice. All the great romantic poets are mythopoeic, are symbolists whose practice must be understood in terms of their attempt to give a total mythic interpretation of the world to which the poet holds the key. The contemporaries of Blake began this revival of mythic poetry — which can be seen even in their interest in Spenser, in *Midsummer Night's Dream* and *The Tempest,* in the devils and witches of Burns, in the interest of Collins in Highland superstitions and their value for the poet, in the pseudo-Norse mythology of Gray, and in the antiquarian researches of Jacob Bryant and Edward Davies. But the first English poet to create a new mythology on a grand scale was Blake. . . .

In Coleridge a theory of symbolism is central; the artist discourses to us by symbols, and nature is a symbolic language. The distinction between symbol and allegory is, in Coleridge, related to that between imagination and fancy (which, in some ways, can be described as a theory of imagery), genius and talent, reason and understanding. In a late discussion he says

that an allegory is but a translation of abstract notions into a picture language, which is itself nothing but an abstraction from objects of sense. On the other hand, a symbol is characterized by a translucence of the special in the individual, or of the general in the special, or of the universal in the general; above all, a symbol is characterized by the translucence of the eternal through and in the temporal. The faculty of symbols is the imagination. . . .

It could be argued that these romantic attitudes, beliefs, and techniques were confined to a small group of great poets and that, on the whole, the England of the early nineteenth century shares many points of view with the Age of Reason. One may grant that the English romantic movement was never as self-conscious or, possibly, as radical as the German or French movements, that eighteenth-century attitudes were far more influential and widespread than on the continent, e.g. in philosophy where utilitarianism and Scottish commonsense philosophy held sway, and that the English romantic theory of poetry is a curious amalgamation of sensualism and associationism, inherited from the eighteenth century and the new or old Platonic idealism. The only major writer who propounded a coherent "idealistic" system was Coleridge, and his "system" or plan for a system was largely an importation from Germany. But there is a good deal of evidence among the minor writers also that the intellectual atmosphere was changing in England. . . . Much research in minor writers and periodicals would be needed to substantiate this fully, but enough evidence has been produced to show that England also underwent the change of intellectual atmosphere which was general in Europe. . . .

One important argument for the coherence and unity of the European romantic movement emerges from an investigation of the minor literatures — the "predictability" of their general character. If we had never heard anything about the Czech romantic movement, it would still be possible, within limits, to assert the presence and absence of certain themes, views, and techniques.

My conclusion concerning the unity of the romantic movement may be distressingly orthodox and even conventional. But it seems necessary to reassert it, especially in view of Lovejoy's famous attack. . . .

I do not, of course, deny differences between the various romantic movements, differences of emphasis and distribution of elements, differences in the pace of development, in the individualities of the great writers. I am perfectly aware that the three groups of ideas I have selected have their historical ancestry before the age of Enlightenment and in undercurrents during the eighteenth century. The view of an organic nature descends from Neoplatonism through Giordano Bruno, Böhme, the Cambridge Platonists, and some passages in Shaftesbury. The view of imagination as creative and of poetry as prophecy has a similar ancestry. A symbolist, and even mythic, conception of poetry is frequent in history, e.g., in the baroque age with its emblematic art, its view of nature as hieroglyphics which man ad [sic!] especially the poet is destined to read. In a sense, romanticism is the revival of something old, but it is a revival with a difference; these ideas were translated into terms acceptable to men who had undergone the experience of the Enlightenment. . . . But for our problem we need only know that there is a difference between the symbol in Pope and in Shelley. This can be described; the change from the type of imagery and symbolism used by Pope to that used by Shelley is an empirical fact of history. It seems difficult to deny that we are confronted with substantially the same fact in noting the difference between Lessing and Novalis or Voltaire and Victor Hugo.

Lovejoy has argued that the "new ideas of the period were in large part heterogeneous, logically independent and sometimes essentially antithetic to one another in their implications." If we look back on our argument, it will be obvious that this view must be mistaken. There is, on the contrary, a profound coherence and mutual implication between the romantic views of nature, imagination, and symbol. Without such a view of nature we could not believe in the significance of symbol and myth. Without symbol and myth the poet would lack the tools for the insight into reality which he claimed, and without such an epistemology, which believes in the creativity of the human mind, there would not be a living nature and a true symbolism. We may not accept this view of the world for ourselves — few of us can accept it literally today — but we should grant that it is coherent and integrated and, as I hope I have shown, all-pervasive in Europe.

We can then go on speaking of romanticism as one European movement, whose slow rise through the eighteenth century we can describe and examine and even call, if we want to, preromanticism. Clearly there are periods of the dominance of a system of ideas and poetic practices; and clearly they have their anticipations and their survivals. To give up these problems because of the difficulties of terminology seems to be tantamount to giving up the central task of literary history. If literary history is not to be content to remain the usual odd mixture of biography, bibliography, anthology, and disconnected emotive criticism, it has to study the total process of literature. This can be done only by tracing the sequence of periods, the rise, dominance, and disintegration of conventions and norms. The term "romanticism" posits all these questions, and that, to my mind, is its best defense.

A Crisis of Faith

BENEDETTO CROCE

Benedetto Croce (1866–1952) was Italy's leading twentieth century philosopher, and one of Italy's most famous liberals. Through the Fascist era and into the post-war period, he was a symbol of dedication to liberal ideals. Much of his philosophic writing was concerned with the philosophy of history, and he also wrote two historical studies dealing with the developments he felt produced the crises of the twentieth century: his *History of Italy, 1871–1915*, and the *History of Europe in the Nineteenth Century*. In his treatment of Romanticism in the latter volume he makes a distinction between theoretic and moral romanticism and ascribes the origin of the latter movement to the difficulty of developing a new faith, the liberal idea, to replace the old beliefs of the preceding era.

THEORETIC and speculative romanticism is the revolt, the criticism, and the attack against literary academicism and philosophic intellectualism, which had dominated in the illuminist age. It awakened the feeling for genuine and great poetry, and set forth the doctrine thereof in the new science of the imagination called aesthetics. It realized the great importance of spontaneity, passion, individuality, and gave them their place in ethics. It knew and made known the right of what exists and operates in all its varieties according to time and place, and founded modern historiography, interpreting it no longer as mockery and derision of past ages, but as understanding of these as parts of the present and of the future. And it reintegrated and retouched all the aspects of history, civil and political history no less than religious, speculative, and artistic. It thrust back into their natural limits the natural and mathematical sciences and their correlative mental form, showing that, outside of their own field, they were impotent to resolve the antinomies with which the mind came into conflict no less than those which had to remain in abstractions and separa-

tions. It grasped life in its active and combative sense, and thus prepared the theoretical premises of liberalism. Even in its irrationalistic concepts, as in the primacy sometimes allotted to emotion and mystic ecstasy, there was a justified polemic against abstract intellectualism, and, in irrational and provisional form, a nucleus of rational truth. . . .

But the romanticism that is spoken of in the practical, sentimental, and moral field is something quite different, belongs to quite a diverse sphere. And if speculative romanticism is resplendent with truth, if the attempts to refute it have always been and always are vain, if it has indeed at various times been judged to be extreme and audacious and yet at the same time never been debased to infirmity, feebleness, and insanity, the other, on the contrary, at once assumed this unhealthy aspect and has always been the object of ethical reproval, more or less stressed, now indulgent and pitying, now severe and satirical, and the necessity has always been felt of treating it and bringing about its cure. The greatest liberators from the chains of intellectualism, the greatest fathers of idealism

From *History of Europe in the Nineteenth Century* by Benedetto Croce, translated by Henry Furst (London, 1934), pp. 42–54. By permission of George Allen & Unwin, Ltd.

and romanticism in critical and speculative concepts, Goethe and Hegel, considered moral romanticism in this fashion, and shrank from it and blamed it, pronouncing it pathological and shameful. Most certainly the praises that later were spent on romanticism, defining it as "protestantism in philosophy" or "liberalism in literature," did not belong to it. . . .

Romanticism was not, as it has so often been interpreted and represented, an effect of the departure from the hereditary and traditional faith, which had yielded certainty and tranquillity of feeling and will; because when an old faith is followed by a new one, the warmth and enthusiasm of the latter covers and makes almost imperceptible the pain and melancholy over the separation and severance from the former. In the eighteenth century society had become widely dechristianized in its intellectual and ruling classes, without any resultant formation of a divided or morbid state of mind, such as romanticism was, and the process even developed with a certain gaiety and cheerfulness. Even the violent rebels against the law, the customs, and the ideas of existing society, the *Stürmer und Dränger,* who for such aspects are considered as proto-romantics, in the achievement of their negations and their rage of destruction gave signs of disordered force rather than of confusion and weakness. But moral romanticism, romanticism as a malady, the *"mal du siècle,"* possessed neither the old nor the new faith, neither the authoritative one of the past nor the clear one of the present, and showed precisely that it was a lack of faith, travailing in eagerness to create one and impotent to do so, or to obtain satisfaction from those which in turn it proclaimed, or to stick to them as principles of thinking and living. . . .

But it was beyond the powers of feminine souls, impressionable, sentimental, incoherent, and voluble, who stimulated and excited in themselves doubts and difficulties that they were not able to master, who loved and courted the dangers in which

they perished. Unable to find their way back to the natural centre that they had questioned, they wandered here and there, clinging now to one point and now to another that could not possibly become a centre. . . .

And so these feminine souls, these "romantics," dreamed of returning to religious transcendence and the peace that it seemed to promise, to the cessation, in silence and in renunciation, of the doubts and anxieties of thought, to the norm accepted because of its very character as a norm that imposes itself and exonerates from all independent solution of the battles waged within the conscience. And as the highest expression of this sort of transcendence and of this imperative ruling was the Catholic faith; not only those who belonged to Catholic peoples and had been brought up from childhood in Catholicism, but also Protestants, Lutherans, or those of other confessions, or even men come from the most distant religions or from no religion at all, became Catholics again or for the first time and even were converted with the due rites, and yet none the less never became intimately or genuinely Catholics, and assumed an ambiguous aspect in the eyes of real Catholics. For this Catholicism of theirs was too rich in sensuousness and imagination, was too eager for colours, music, singing, ancient cathedrals, figures of Madonnas and saints, cradled itself too fondly in the pleasures of sin, in penitence and tears; in regard to dogma it did, in truth, give itself ultra-Catholic airs, but was not equally obedient and faithful to the Roman pontiff and to his decrees and his policy. They called themselves or believed themselves anti-Protestant, but in such a way that they could not refrain from frequent allusions to the necessity for a new form or for a reform that should be fundamentally Catholic, but should resolve within itself the dissonances of Protestantism and Catholicism. Others, or the same ones, would at times be seized by rage against Catholicism, or even against Christianity, and turn to championing a restored paganism, opposing to the figure of the Holy Virgin that of the goddess Venus, now the Hellenic one, now the Germanic-mediaeval. Others, attracted by the studies, initiated at this time, of Oriental languages and literature, borrowed from them ideas of ancient rites, or compounded eclectically new and bizarre ones, or recurred to the practice of magic. Others, last of all, flung themselves into a sort of pantheism, adoring Nature, losing themselves in the sensations that she seemed to provide them, and returning, as they liked to say, to the primitive religion of the Germanic peoples.

Those who were more metaphysically or sacerdotally disposed were followed, and often joined, by those who enjoyed a more erotic tone, who sought for redemption in love and for divinity in the beloved lady, not so much with a revival of motifs that had belonged to the *stil nuovo* of the thirteenth century and to the Platonism of the Renaissance, as with a refinement and sublimation of sensuality, which is the kernel of the romantic religion of love. . . . There was pathos in the series of expectations, ecstasies, inebriations and disappointments and despair, from which, however, would always arise again the idea of this form of love and of this feminine figure, which would descend from time to time to crown with a heavenly nimbus the blond or dark head of this or that earthly woman, encountered on the earthly path.

In other spirits, or at other moments, the bent of the imagination was preponderantly ethical and political — "political fantasy" because "romantic politics," that is, a politics of the romantic malady, is a contradiction in terms — and in this case belief and happiness were sought for in social modes of living differing from the present ones and particularly in the restoration of past ages. And as the immediate past, that of the *ancien régime,* was still too clearly remembered, was too precise in its limits, and did not easily lend itself to idealization and sacred sublimation, their desire was transferred to the remoter past. Meanwhile learning had re-established the continuity of historical development, and investigated and better understood the Middle Ages, and so they turned to the mediaeval period, in which they saw or thought they saw shadows as solid figures, marvels of fidelity, loyalty, purity, generosity, discipline and lack of discipline at the same time, and what was constant alternating with what was unexpected, simplicity of life in a small and peaceful circle with the charm of adventures throughout the vast unknown world that was full of surprises. To this religion of the Middle Ages we owe the more or less academic restorations of old castles and old cathedrals, the false Gothic that raged everywhere in Europe, the false poetry that in dilettante fashion set itself to imitating the mediaeval forms of epic, lyric, and miracle plays, romances telling of knights and tourneys, chatelaines and enamoured pages, minstrels and clowns, romantic masquerades. . . .

But if the religion of the Middle Ages was the main one and the most widely spread, it was not the only one; and next to it, and sharing the honours with it, there rose and towered the religion of the race and the nation, of that nation which, because of scanty information and historic reflection, was considered the creative and dominant race of the Middle Ages, the Germanic, whose courage was now being sought for and discovered and celebrated in every part of Europe — where, historically speaking, should rather have been found, as a common foundation, the Romanic peoples, which for the first time gave it unity and consciousness. . . .

Other religions of an ethical and political tendency also had their more or less numerous devotees, such as that idyllic return to nature and the country and the simple peasant's garb in which there breathed the inspiration of one of its principal precursors, Rousseau; and, opposed to it, the tendency to the stormy, the enraged, the titanic, in which persisted instead the impulse of *Stürm und Dräng.* But above all worthy of notice, because of its capacity for proselytizing and the various off-shoots that it sent out, was the aestheticizing conception, of life to be lived as passion and imagination, beauty and poetry. . . .

All these, considered in their source, were perversions, inasmuch as they substituted the particular for the universal, the contingent for the eternal, the creature for the creator. But into such diverse and complicated and intricate sentiments there crept also those which are more appropriately called perversions, that is, not only exaggerations and usurpations but somersaults of values: lust and sensuality set in the place of ideality, the cruel and the horrible savoured with voluptuousness, the taste for incest, sadism, Satanism, and other like delights, at the same time monstrous and stupid; as can be seen or divined in poets and men of letters even of the very highest class, such as Chateaubriand, Byron, Shelley, in whom, fortunately, there is not only this, and even this exists as a rule in incidental or evanescent fashion.

Here we do not mean to pause and portray in its varied combinations and gradations, which run to infinity, the "mal du siècle," which moreover has often been portrayed, with more or less skill, by others; for all that was needed was merely to explain its genesis in relation to the philosophy and the religion of liberty. This genesis, as we have seen, lay in its impotence to appropriate to itself this philosophy and religion, although at the same time it took from it a few elements, which promptly corrupted it, and falsified historicity by sentimentalizing over the past and by leanings towards restoration, nationality by the fanaticism of race, liberty by egoarchy and anarchy, and the value of poetry to life by poetry-life and life-poetry. But we must not, on the other hand, ignore all — and it was much — that the liberal faith was able to influence in this romanticism, nor the way in which, according to the various cases, it transcended it or hemmed it in or subdued it to itself in varying degrees. . . .

Moral romanticism operated in the midst of a growth of generous hopes, intentions, and works that confined it, tempered it, and often turned it towards the good. Superior spirits, taking part as they did in the drama of their time, did indeed suffer from this malady, but as from a growing-sickness, from which they recovered and from which they drew fruits of experience, powers of discipline, a capacity for a wider human understanding. And from their midst emerged the keenest judges and the severest critics of romanticism, such as Goethe, whom we have mentioned before, who defined romantic poetry as "hospital poetry" and manifested his aversion to the "sentimental people" who, when they are put to the test, always fail and show themselves to be little and bad, and Hegel, whom we also mentioned, who uttered the most caustic satire and the most varied analysis of romantic fatuity and vanity, up to which he held, so that they might gaze upon themselves as in a magic mirror, the good and savoury prose of real life with its unwearying activity, its physiological pains and physiological joys.

To be sure, not a few romantics, those who could never succeed either in overcoming and calming the uproar they had excited in their own breasts or in eliminating it by forgetting it and resuming their modest everyday lives, went to rack and ruin. Some of them ended in madness and physical suicide, others in moral suicide, in debauches or the insincere practice of a religion that was not serious and not felt. The greater part of them, in inactivity and groaning in solitude and ennui, were like Byron's Manfred, who spoke of himself as "averse from life" and who might have been (says someone who watches him) a noble creature and was instead

an awful chaos — light and darkness —
And mind and dust — and passions and pure thought
Mix'd, and contending without end or order. . . .

In general, the romantic features are very strongly marked in all the men of that age, as can be seen in their letters and biographies, and even, almost, by merely looking at their portraits, with the characteristic look, the hairdress, the pose, and the cut of the garments. And if in some countries where the feeling and the activity for liberty did not stand in the forefront, the romantics (who politically were nothing, because they were simply never-sick and fancy-sick) were able, by their words of consent or dissent, by the manifestations of their humour or ill-humour, to pass as conservatives and reactionaries among the peoples whose hearts beat with a quicker rhythm, in whom the idea and the flower of the intellectuals were liberal, yet their name soon became synonymous with "liberal," and priests and police suspected and kept an eye on romantic youth. The sorrow of the world, the mystery of the universe, the impetus towards the sublimity of love and heroism, the desolation and the despair over desired and unattainable beatitude, the walks under the friendly moon, the Hamlet-like visits to cemeteries, the romantic beards and curls, the romantic style, these and other like things furnished evidence of unruly spirits, of whom it was to be expected and feared that they might conspire in the factions and rise in arms as soon as occasion presented itself.

A New Sensibility

MARIO PRAZ

Mario Praz is an Italian scholar and critic, who has taught English studies in Italy and Italian studies in Britain. His concern is primarily for comparative literature in the modern era, with special emphasis upon the nineteenth century. Besides his book *The Romantic Agony*, from which the following selection is drawn, he has written *The Hero in Eclipse in Victorian Fiction*. Praz takes issue with those who, like Lovejoy, doubt the usefulness of the general term "romantic" and argues for its continued employment as an *historical* category, in the treatment of a form of sensibility in the arts. In the latter connection he disagrees with Croce's view that Romanticism involved a metaphysical problem derived from a loss of faith, preferring to attribute the origin of the new sensibility to new techniques in the arts.

In the opinion of Croce, who in any case fails to break away in this matter from the usual method of literary historians . . . the root of Romanticism *qua* moral phenomenon, of the "mal du siècle," has to be sought in the borderland between an ancient, hereditary faith which had collapsed, and a new faith, the faith in new philosophical and liberal ideals which had as yet been only imperfectly and partially digested. . . .

What could be more obvious than the attempt to trace the sources of the aberrations of a period to a metaphysical crisis? As an example of this, it will be remembered that literary historians, wishing to account for the rise in England of that peculiar poetical current which started with John Donne, attributed it to the collapse of the medieval conception of the world beneath the reiterated blows of newly-acquired knowledge, with the undermining of dogmas which resulted.

Now, though I do not deny that such explanations are worthy of consideration, it seems to me that they account only very indirectly for particular tendencies of sensibility. At most they limit the screen on which the visions are projected, but they do not say why exactly those visions, and not others, appear. The course followed by currents of religious faith (including among these philosophy) is different from the course through which the education of sensibility is accomplished. . . . The cult of "Medusean" beauty burst forth into a fashion in the nineteenth century but isolated signs of it were not lacking even earlier, which indicate that it was a case of a sporadic germ which at a certain moment became epidemic. The period of greatest violence may have coincided with a religious crisis, but this only avails to explain the intensity, not the nature of the epidemic, which arrived at its final form by quite a different process.

If, therefore, the history of ideas and ideals during the nineteenth century constitutes a necessary frame for the picture I have painted, it is a part which completes, rather than conditions, the whole; there was no obligation for me to examine it afresh, nor to deal with phenomena of other kinds, which in any case have been fully discussed by others.

Why was it that, towards the end of the

From *The Romantic Agony* by Mario Praz, translated from the Italian by Angus Davidson, London, 1933 (pp. x–xii, 1–3, 5–7, 9, 11–15). By permission of the Oxford University Press.

eighteenth century, people came to consider landscape with different eyes? why did they look for a "je ne sais quoi" which they had not looked for before? Why, at about the same time, did the "beauty of the horrid" become a source, no longer of conceits, as in the seventeenth century, but of sensations? To such questions adequate answers are not to be found in the history of the religious, philosophical, moral and practical development of the period. In this field of ideas is to be found a confirmation of the axiom propounded by Wilde, as to Nature imitating Art (in *The Decay of Lying*). Education of sensibility came about through works of art; what it is therefore chiefly important to establish is the means by which the transmission of themes from one artist to another is effected. The mysterious bond between pleasure and suffering has certainly always existed; it is one of the *vulnera naturae* which is as old as man himself. But it became the common inheritance of Romantic and Decadent sensibility through a particular chain of literary influences. . . .

. . "ROMANTIC"; AN APPROXIMATE TERM

The epithet "romantic" and the antithetical terms "classic" and "romantic" are approximate labels which have long been in use. The philosopher solemnly refuses to allow them, exorcising them with unerring logic, but they creep quietly in again and are always obtruding themselves, elusive, tiresome, indispensable; the grammarian attempts to give them their proper status, their rank and fixed definition, but in spite of all his laborious efforts he discovers that he has been treating shadows as though they were solid substance.

Like an infinite number of other words in current usage, these approximate terms have a value and answer a useful purpose, provided that they are treated at their proper value — that is, as approximate terms — and that what they cannot give — exact and cogent definition of thought — is not demanded of them. They are serviceable makeshifts, and their fictitious character can be easily proved, but if the proof of their relatively arbitrary nature should cause us to dispense with their services, I do not see that literary history would benefit by it.

The case is similar to that of literary "genres." Let them be abolished: soon they will crop up again in the shape of more elaborate distinctions and categories, more in accordance with the spirit of the particular moment, but no less approximate. . . .

Literary criticism assumes the existence of a history of culture — the culture of a particular *milieu* or of a particular individual. If the merging of the work of art into the general history of culture results in losing sight of the individual artist, it is impossible, on the other hand, to think of the latter without recurring to the former. Tendencies, themes, and mannerisms current in a writer's own day provide an indispensable aid to the interpretation of his work. True, for the purpose of aesthetic appreciation, this work forms a unique world shut up in itself, rounded off and perfected, an *individuum ineffabile*; but this philosophical truism would leave the critic no other alternative but a mystical, admiring silence.

But there is more to it than that. If it is true that the life of a work of art is in direct ratio to its being, so to speak, eternally contemporary, or able to reflect, with a universal application, the sentiments of periods in history which are in themselves diverse and remote, it is yet true that, in separating the work of art from its own particular cultural substratum, it is easy to fall into arbitrary, fantastic interpretations which alter the nature of the work even to the extent of making it unrecognizable. How many variations on Dante and Shakespeare have not been devised by critics of creative rather than historical minds? . . .

Now the use of formulas such as "romantic," "baroque," etc., serves to give some guidance to the interpretation of a work of art, or, in other words, to define the limits within which the activity of the critic is to be confined and beyond which lie mere arbitrary and anachronistic judgments. The sole object of these formulas is to keep in mind the character of the period in which the work was produced, in such a way as to avoid the danger of a combination of words, sounds, colours or forms becoming surreptitiously invested with ideas which are aroused in the mind of the interpreter, but which certainly did not exist in the mind of the artist. Similar results may arise out of very different artistic intentions. Thus in a seventeenth century writer like Alessandro Adimari one finds a love-sonnet on a beautiful lady recently buried, but one must be careful not to see in it a manifestation of romantic necrophily; when elsewhere, he goes into ecstacies over a "wounded beauty," one must refrain from imagining in such a composition a morbid exquisiteness of feeling such as is found in Baudelaire's *Une Martyre*; but keeping in mind the partiality of the baroque period for every form of wit, one must attribute the choice of these unattractive subjects mainly to the desire of provoking astonishment through the conceit which can be elicited from them. . . .

Approximate terms such as "baroque," "romantic," "decadent," etc., have their origins in definite revolutions of sensibility, and it serves no purpose to detach them from their historical foundations and apply them generously to artists of varied types, according to the more or less extravagant whims of critics. It happens only too often that the unsuccessful artist which lurks repressed in the soul of the critic seeks an outlet in the composition of a critical novel, or in projecting on some author or other a light which is quite alien to him, which alters his appearance and brings it up to date, greatly to the detriment of the correct interpretation. For such purposes are these approximate terms used capriciously by critics, just as a clever cook uses sauces and seasonings to disguise the food. . . . These terms, however, are intended merely to indicate where the accent falls, and have no meaning outside the circumference of certain historical periods. . . . Hence the highly problematic value of any research into the forerunners of seventeenth-century literature, of Romanticism, of Futurism — a form of research which is as elegantly literary as it is generally arbitrary and inconclusive, since these empirical formulas cannot be applied to every period and every place. It is, I believe, to the neglect of this criterion that one may ascribe the discredit into which certain of these terms have fallen, particularly the antithetical terms, "classic" and "romantic."

These two terms, introduced, as is well known, by Goethe and Schiller, have ended by being adopted as the criteria of interpretation for all periods and all literatures; in the case of literature, as well as in that of the plastic arts and music, people frequently speak of Classic and Romantic in the same way as, in politics, they speak, universally, of Conservative and Liberal, with an extension of meaning which is, quite obviously, arbitrary. . . .

However, if one wishes to protect the useful function of the word "romantic" as an approximate term, one must first of all distinguish this function from that of its so-called opposite "classic," which has become nothing more than a secondary abstract reflection of the term "romantic": then returning to the original use of the word, one must accept it as the definition of a peculiar kind of sensibility at a fixed historical period. The indiscriminate use of the word can only cause misunderstanding and confusion, as it does when Grierson speaks of the "romantic thrill" one feels when reading the myths of the Cave, of Er, and of the Chariot of the Soul in the *Phaedrus*, and of the "romantic conception" of Plato "of an ideal world behind the visible"; here the epithet "romantic" is surreptitiously transferred from the modern reader's impression to the Platonic conception itself, and Plato is shown as a Romantic because the reader is pleased to interpret his legends in a romantic way. . . .

. . . Classicism, then, is a phenomenon by no means alien to the romantic spirit;

on the contrary, inasmuch as it seeks to revive manners and ideas belonging to the past, inasmuch as it strives longingly toward a fantastic pagan world, rather than sharing in the state of serene equilibrium proper to so-called classical works of art (which are serene without knowing it), it shares in the same spiritual travail which is usually defined as characteristically and *par excellence* "romantic." It is not the content which decides whether a work should be labelled "romantic" or not, but the spirit, and, in this sense, a Holderlin or a Keats, worshipping, as they do, a vanished world, is no less romantic than a Coleridge or a Shelley. In other words, there is such a thing as a "Romantic Movement," and classicism is only an aspect of it. There is no opposite pole to "romantic," merely because "romantic" indicates a certain state of sensibility which, simply, is different from any other, and not comparable either by co-ordination or by contrast.

How can one describe the new state of sensibility which came into full flower towards the end of the eighteenth century? What does "romantic" mean? . . .

The word "romantic" appears for the first time in the English language about the middle of the seventeenth century, meaning "like the old romances," and shows how there began to be felt, about this time, a real need to give names to certain characteristics of the chivalrous and pastoral romances. These characteristics, thrown into relief by contrast with the growing rationalistic spirit which was soon to triumph in Pope and Dr. Johnson, lay in the falsity, the unreality, the fantastic and irrational nature of events and sentiments described in these romances. . . .

But a new current in taste can be discerned right from the beginning of the eighteenth century: there is a growing tendency to recognize the importance of imagination in works of art. "Romantic," though continuing to mean something slightly absurd, takes on the flavour of *attractive*, suited to please the imagination. . . . Side by side with the depreciatory use of the word in relation to the events and sentiments of the old romances, "romantic" came to be used to describe scenes and landscapes similar to those described in them, and, this time, without any note of scorn. . . . In this second sense, the adjective has gradually ceased to retain its connection with the literary *genre* (the romances) from which it was originally derived, and has come to express more and more the growing love for wild and melancholy aspects of nature. It is so closely connected with certain qualities of landscape that French translators of English books of the period, when the word "romantic" is used, often render it with "pittoresque": which shows that the French were not yet aware of the new state of sensibility suggested by the word "romantic." . . . In *romantique* Rousseau found the appropriate word to define that elusive and indistinct thing which hitherto he had vaguely expressed by "je ne sais quoi." . . . In this sense, "romantic" assumes a subjective character, like "interesting," "charming," "exciting," which describe not so much the property of the objects as our reactions to them, the effect which they arouse in an impressionable onlooker. Besides, as L. P. Smith observes, Nature described as "romantic" is seen through a veil of associations and feelings extracted from poetry and literature in general.

The term *pittoresque*, which arose at the same time, expresses a similar phenomenon. The subjective element, implicit in "romantic," rendered this word particularly suitable to describe the new kind of literature in which suggestion and aspiration had so large a part. . . . *Magie der Einbildungskraft* (Magic of the Imagination) is the title of a well-known essay in which Jean Paul defines the essence of romantic sensibility. How does it come about — asks Jean Paul — that everything which exists only in aspiration . . . and in remembrance, everything which is remote, dead, unknown, possesses this magic transfiguring charm? Because — the answer is — everything, when inwardly represented, loses its precise outline, since the imagination possesses the magic virtue of making things infinite. . . .

The word "romantic" thus comes to be associated with another group of ideas, such as "magic," "suggestive," "nostalgic," and above all with words expressing states of mind which cannot be described, such as the German "Sehnsucht" and the English "wistful." It is curious to note that these two words have no equivalent in the Romance languages — a clear sign of the Nordic, Anglo-Germanic origin of the sentiments they express. Such ideas have this in common, that they furnish only a vague indication, leaving it to the imagination to make the final evocation. A Freudian would say that these ideas appeal to the unconscious in us. It is the appeal of Yeats' *Land of Heart's Desire.*

The essense of Romanticism consequently comes to consist in that which cannot be described. The word and the form, says Schlegel in *Lucinde,* are only accessories. The essential is the thought and the poetic image, and these are rendered possible only in a passive state. The Romantic exalts the artist who does not give a material form to his dreams — the poet ecstatic in front of a forever blank page, the musician who listens to the prodigious concerts of his soul without attempting to translate them into notes. It is romantic to consider concrete expression as a decadence, a contamination. How many times has the magic of the ineffable been celebrated, from Keats, with his

Heard melodies are sweet, but those unheard
Are sweeter. . . .

to Maeterlinck, with his theory that silence is more musical than any sound.

But these are extreme cases, in which the romantic tends to merge with the mystical. The normal is that of suggestive expression, which evokes more than it states. Whenever we encounter such a method, we do not hesitate to define the artist who makes use of it as "romantic." But the legitimate use of this term depends upon the deliberate method of the artist, not upon the mere interpretation of the reader. . . .

EXPLANATIONS OF ROMANTICISM

The Need for New Symbols

REGINALD A. FOAKES

The British critic and literary scholar, R. A. Foakes, identifies Romanticism as a response to the need for developing new symbols in an era bereft of the certainties its predecessors had possessed, suggesting a position between those of Croce and Praz.

THE Romantic poets wrote for a world which had changed greatly since the sixteenth, even since the early eighteenth century. Poets of these earlier times had been able to assume as their frame of reference a concept of an ordered and stable universe, organized in a system of degree ranging from God through angels, men and beasts to inanimate objects, a system in which man was the link between the natural and divine worlds, and in which the hierarchal structure of society corresponded to the ordered arrangement of the universe. This order did not exist in actuality, though it provided a prop or succedaneum for Tudor despotism, and might be seen as an ideal which society should attempt to fulfil; and indeed, much of the greatest literature of these centuries seems to grow out of the tensions between the ideal concept and the failure of life to correspond to it. . . .

However, the concept of order provided a frame of reference for literature. Actions, ideas, relationships of characters, were inevitably posed against an ordering of the world, a religious ordering in as much as it led up to God, which established their value and distinguished clearly between right and wrong, good and bad. Any story tended to acquire symbolic or allegorical significance in the light of this concept, and could be used to embody profound ideas and feelings about man and the world, could become topical in the largest sense. It is significant that most literature prior to the middle of the eighteenth century tells a story, or at least says what it has to say in terms of a world, events and people outside the author himself.

The concept of order was apprehended, it was thought, by the reason, which was regarded as the principal human faculty, the one which distinguished man from beasts, and which he shared with angels. Man, fallen since Adam fell, struggled to attain self-knowledge, and thence knowledge of God. The faculties of the rational soul, the reason, or power of judging between good and evil, truth and falsity, and the understanding, the power of comprehending things intelligible but not material, ideas, including the idea of God, had to be employed constantly to keep the senses in check and control the will, depraved since Adam. . . . In a healthy mind the reason controlled the operations of the senses, and it was thought that the imagination, that "general source of all our evils and disorderly passions," on receiv-

From *The Romantic Assertion* by Reginald A. Foakes (London, 1958), pp. 39–48. By permission of the Yale University Press and Methuen and Co. Ltd.

ing impressions from the senses, "changeth and rechangeth, mingleth and vnmingleth," coins all sorts of new and monstrous images, and is as easily receptive of the devil's illusions as of heavenly visions. It was regarded as a faculty men share with beasts, whereas reason was the prerogative of human beings; but as the mind of man was quicker than that of beasts, so his imagination worked to greater effect

so that in trueth, *fantasie* [i.e. imagination] is a very dangerous thing. For if it bee not guided and brideled by reason, it troubleth and mooueth all the sense and vnderstanding, as a tempest doeth the sea.

By the end of the eighteenth century the disparity between the ideal order and the world in which men lived had become so great, the ideal so meaningless, as to destroy its usefulness even as a myth. The growth of the middle class, of industry and trade, the decline of the monarchy and the aristocracy as representatives of power, and the approach of democracy were capped, for the early Romantic poets at any rate, by the French Revolution, Godwin's notions of a perfect society as a blithe anarchy, and pantisocracy. The old concept of an external order in the universe had gone, and was replaced by various ideas, which, like Godwin's theory, postulated the possibility of the self-fulfilment of the individual man as an ideal — the natural corollary to democracy; so Coleridge, welcoming the revolution, cried

And lo! the Great, the Rich, the Mighty Men,
The Kings and the Chief Captains of the
    World,
With all that fixed on high like stars of
    Heaven
Shot baleful influence, shall be cast to
    earth . . .
Return pure Faith! return meek Piety!
The kingdoms of the world are your's:
    each heart
Self-governed, the vast family of Love
Raised from the common earth by common
    toil

Enjoy the equal produce.
        (*Religious Musings*, 309–12, 339–43)

The Romantic poets wrote for a society which could no longer be measured against a concept of order and degree, or by the standards of a mode of government fixed in a religious dispensation, one which was beginning to postulate the notion of self-government, of the equality of men. The destruction of an external frame of reference led them to seek a principle of order within the individual, within themselves, to write of man and the world largely in terms of their own inner life, or their own self-sought, self-created relationship with God. The point of reference in their poetry is the individual rather than society, or society seen as a collection of individuals, and not as an ordered hierarchy, and many of their greatest poems are documents of their own lives, *The Prelude, Don Juan, In Memoriam.*

The principle of order they sought was established not in terms of the external world and an appeal to reason, but in terms of the inner world of the individual, and an appeal to imagination. New critical attitudes and criteria were formulated to interpret and defend the new poetry, and received their finest expression in Coleridge's *Biographia Literaria* (1817). His theory of the imagination as the supreme unifying and creative power in the poet, was one aspect of a transcendentalism much less emphasized by modern writers who base their critical outlook on his; the imagination for Coleridge was that faculty which idealizes and unifies, the faculty by which we may perceive the unity of the universe, and apprehend God. It is not through Reason and self-knowledge that we approach the divine, but through the highest form of self-consciousness, which "is for *us* the source and principle of all *our* possible knowledge." It is through the individual consciousness, represented at its highest in the creative act of the imagination which repeats the eternal act of creation of God, that we perceive God;

self-consciousness is not a kind of *being*, but a kind of *knowing*, and that too the highest and farthest that exists for *us*.

This highest form of knowledge is possible only to a few, and only those who

can acquire the philosophic imagination, the sacred power of self-intuition,

will know and feel the "potential" working in them, will be endowed with "the ascertaining vision, the intuitive knowledge." The best poetry will have the quality of intuitive perception of larger unities, and will represent the highest form of self-consciousness of the particular poet. It then becomes permissible to judge a poem critically as an expression of an individual mind, an inner experience, and to define critical values in terms of "originality" or "inspiration," concepts commonly used to acknowledge the presence of some mode of intuitive perception. . . .

The concept of ideal order in human society, the world of man, which had provided Shakespeare and Pope with a frame of reference, had collapsed and could no longer supply images of harmony for the Romantic poets; indeed, as stress was laid on self-intuition, self-consciousness and the individual imagination, human society became an image of waste, futility and ultimate disorder — so in Romantic and Victorian poetry the city becomes an image of spiritual exhaustion, or even an image of hell. The natural world also lost its order and its old emblematic function of providing a set of correspondences to the world of man, and took on a new aspect, offering in its wildness, as untainted by man, a refuge from disorder, and in its grandeurs, types of the sublime, images of aspiration. Natural objects, which seemed pure and permanent, or permanently recurring, in relation to the corruption of society and the transitoriness of life, were translated into symbols of the Romantic search for order, or into images of a spiritual harmony. Whereas for Shakespeare and Pope the natural world had reflected the order and

values of man's world, of human society, an order attributed, it is true, to a divine dispensation, it now came to be used to embody the aspiration of the Romantic poet, to reflect directly a transcendental or spiritual order established by the imagination. . . .

Whereas Shakespeare and Pope could use an accepted frame of reference as a touchstone of values, the Romantic poet had to employ his imagination to create one, and he wrote his greatest poetry when he succeeded in giving birth to a "system of symbols" conducting truths. These might not even be truths of the same kind as those which Shakespeare and Pope embody in poetry, for the natural order to which these refer was taken as a norm *from* which the world and society (man in his fallen state) deviate in error or rebellion; but the Romantic poet attempted to establish a harmony such as the individual isolated in an anarchic society might attain by the power of self-intuition, that is, a possible spiritual order in which the individual might find an ideal, find repose from the world, and *into* which he might deviate from the norm. Since there was no common frame of reference to which the Romantic poet's system of symbols could be related, the truths which they might conduct were not always apparent, as is instanced by the famous review of *The Rime of the Ancient Mariner* as "the strangest story of a cock and a bull." This difficulty was overcome in two ways, firstly by the use of images of impression, and secondly by the use of a vocabulary of value-words attached to these images.

By employing images of impression from the natural world, the poet could rely on traditional and common associations to enforce a symbolic value, and could use, to cite two simple examples, the rose as a type of beauty, mountains as emblems of aspiration. Inevitably some images proved so appropriate to the Romantic endeavour to tame chaos, to assert an ideal order, that they recur in the work of many poets. . . .

Light is one of many natural phenomena which provided images for the Romantic poets; indeed, all the forms of nature served as types of a permanence contrasting with the mutability of human life. . . . This "bright Reality," of the light that is a symbol of love and the intuitive experience of harmony, and is associated with the beneficial forms of nature, with all that is fertile or helps towards fertility, has its opposite in images of darkness, chaos and barrenness, amongst which the most important is perhaps that of the city. . . . The city is peopled by savages, and the noble shepherds of Wordsworth's poetry are corrupted by contact with societies of men and cities. The poet called London a "wide waste" in *The Prelude*; for the order, the harmony, which the Romantic poets assert is not one of society, but a transcendental harmony which the individual can attain only through communion with fit symbols, with what is beautiful and permanent, finding "religious meanings in the forms of Nature."

Another means these poets employed to establish this transcendental order was a vocabulary of assertion, of value-words representing concepts or feelings universally regarded as valuable, such as beauty, truth, liberty; words representative of the highest kind of bond between human beings, such as love, sympathy, harmony; words endowed by religious associations with a special sanctity, such as grace, ministry; or again, words expressive of the greatest human endeavour and aspiration, such as power, might, awful, sublime. These words and others which in their common use were associated with what men most value, with the loftiest hopes and ambitions, the greatest achievements, were used by the poets in connexion with images of impression. This vocabulary provided a context of values for the images, which take on a special character in terms of the value-words, for aspects of the natural world are endowed with the noblest human and religious attributes by their means. . . .

A Flight from Reality

ARNOLD HAUSER

Arnold Hauser is an Hungarian born art historian who is now a British subject. He was trained in German scholarship, and his work reveals the influence of such major German sociologists as Max Weber and Georg Simmel. He views art and literature as sociological problems, and in the following selection from his monumental *The Social History of Art* he ascribes Romanticism to the desire to flee from a chaotic social reality, a view directly contradictory to that of Barzun.

GERMAN AND WESTERN ROMANTICISM

Nineteenth-century liberalism identified romanticism with the Restoration and reaction. There may have been a certain justification for this emphasis, especially in Germany, but in general it led to a false conception of the historical process. It was not corrected until scholars began to distinguish between German and Western romanticism and to derive the one from reactionary and the other from progressive tendencies. The resulting picture certainly came much nearer to the truth but still contained a considerable simplification of the facts, for, from a political point of view, neither the one nor the other form of romanticism was clear and consistent. In the end a distinction was made, in accordance with the real situation, between an early and a later phase both in German and in French and English romanticism, a romanticism of the first and another of the second generation. It was ascertained that the development followed different directions in Germany and Western Europe and that German romanticism proceeded from its originally revolutionary attitude to a reactionary standpoint, whereas Western romanticism proceeded from a monarchist-conservative point of view to liberalism.

This account of the situation was intrinsically correct, but it did not prove to be particularly fruitful for the task of defining romanticism. The characteristic feature of the romantic movement was not that it stood for a revolutionary or an anti-revolutionary, a progressive or a reactionary ideology, but that it reached both positions by a fanciful, irrational and undialectical route. Its evolutionary enthusiasm was based just as much on ignorance of the ways of the world as its conservatism, its enthusiasm for the "Revolution, Fichte, and Goethe's *Wilhelm Meister*" was just as ingenuous, just as remote from an appreciation of the real motives behind the historical issues, as its frenzied devotion to the Church and the Crown, to chivalry and feudalism. Perhaps events themselves would have taken a different turn, if the intelligentsia had not, even in France, left it to others to think and act realistically. Everywhere there was a romanticism of the Revolution, just as there was a romanticism of the Counter-Revolution and the Restoration. The Dantons and the Robespierres were just as unrealistic dogmatists as the Chateaubriands and the de Maistres, the Goerres and Adam Muellers. Friedrich Schlegel was a romantic in his youth with his enthusiasm for Fichte, *Wilhelm Meister,* and the Revolution, as he was in his old age with his enthusiasm for Metternich and the Holy Alliance. But Metternich himself was no romantic, despite his conservatism and traditionalism; he left it to the literary men to consolidate the mythos of historicism, legitimism and clericalism. A realist is a man who knows when he is fighting for his own interests and when he is making concessions to those of others; and a dialectician is one who is aware that the historical situation at any given moment consists of a complex of different irreducible motives and tasks. Despite all his appreciation of the past, the romantic judges his own time unhistorically, undialectically; he does not grasp that it stands midway between the past and the future and represents an indissoluble conflict of static and dynamic elements.

Goethe's definition, according to which romanticism embodies the principle of disease — a verdict that is hardly to be accepted in the way it was meant — gains a new significance and a new confirmation in the light of modern psychology. For, if romanticism, in fact, sees only one side of a total situation fraught with tension and conflict, if it always considers only one factor in the dialectic of history and stresses this at the expense of the other, if, finally, such a one-sidedness, such an exaggerated, over-compensating reaction, betrays a lack of spiritual balance, then romanticism can rightly be called "diseased." Why should one exaggerate and distort things, if one does not feel disturbed and frightened by them? "Things and actions are what they are, and the consequences of them will be what they will be; why then should we wish to be deceived?" says Bishop Butler, and thereby gives the best description of the serene and "healthy" eighteenth-century sense of reality with its aversion to all illusion. From this realistic point of view, romanticism always seems a lie, a self-deception, which, as Nietzsche says in reference to Wagner, "does not want to conceive antitheses as antitheses," and shouts

the loudest about what it doubts the most profoundly. The escape to the past is only one form of romantic unreality and illusionism — there is also an escape into the future, into Utopia. What the romantic clings to is, in the final analysis, of no consequence, the essential thing is his fear of the present and of the end of the world.

Romanticism was not only of epoch-making importance, it was also aware of its importance. It represented one of the most decisive turning points in the history of the European mind, and it was perfectly conscious of its historical rôle. Since the Gothic, the development of sensibility had received no stronger impulse and the artist's right to follow the call of his feelings and individual disposition had probably never been emphasized with such absoluteness. The rationalism that had been steadily progressing since the Renaissance, and was given a position of dominating importance in the whole civilized world by the enlightenment, suffered the most painful setback in its history. Never since the dissolution of the supernaturalism and traditionalism of the Middle Ages had reason, alertness and sobriety of mind, the will to and the capacity for self-control, been spoken of with such contempt. "Those who restrain desire do so because theirs is weak enough to be restrained" — as is said even by Blake, who was in no sense in agreement with the uncontrolled emotionalism of a Wordsworth. Rationalism, as a principle of science and practical affairs, soon recovered from the romantic onslaught, but European art has remained "romantic." Romanticism was not merely a universal European movement, seizing one nation after another and creating a universal literary language which was finally just as intelligible in Russia and Poland as in England and France, it also proved to be one of those trends which, like the naturalism of the Gothic or the classicism of the Renaissance, have remained a lasting factor in the development of art. There is, in fact, no product of modern art, no emotional impulse, no impression or mood of the modern man, which does not owe its delicacy and variety to the sensitiveness which developed out of romanticism. The whole exuberance, anarchy and violence of modern art, its drunken, stammering lyricism, its unrestrained, unsparing exhibitionism, is derived from it. . . .

The whole nineteenth century was artistically dependent on romanticism, but romanticism itself was still a product of the eighteenth century and never lost the consciousness of its transitional and historically problematical character. Western Europe had gone through several other — similar and more serious — crises, but it had never had so much the feeling of having reached a turning point in its development. This was by no means the first time that a generation had taken a critical attitude to its own historical background and rejected the traditional patterns of culture, because it was unable to express its own outlook on life in them. Previous generations had had the feeling of growing old and the desire for renewal, but to none had it occurred to make a problem of the meaning and *raison d'être* of its own culture and to ask whether it was entitled to its own frame of mind and whether it represented a necessary link in the total chain of human culture. The romantic feeling of rebirth was by no means new; the Renaissance had already experienced it and even the Middle Ages had toyed with ideas of renewal and visions of resurrection of which ancient Rome had been the theme. But no generation had had such a strong awareness of being the heir and descendant of previous ages, none had had so decidedly the desire simply to repeat and to awaken to new life a past age and a lost culture. . . . It is unmistakable that the romantic experience of history gives expression to a psychotic fear of the present and an attempt to escape into the past. But no psychosis has ever been more fruitful. Romanticism owes it its historical sensitivity and clairvoyance, its feeling for relationships, however remote and however difficult to interpret. Without this hypersensitiveness, it would hardly have succeeded in restoring the great historical continuities of culture, in marking the boundary between modern culture and classical antiquity, in recognizing in Christianity the great dividing line in the history of the West and discovering the common "romantic" nature of all the individualistic, reflective, problematical cultures derived from Christianity.

Without the historical consciousness of romanticism, without the constant questioning of the meaning of the present, by which the thinking of the romantics was dominated, the whole historicism of the nineteenth century and one of the deepest revolutions in the history of the human mind would have been inconceivable. In spite of Heraclitus and the Sophists, the nominalism of scholastic philosophy and the naturalism of the Renaissance, the dynamic approach of capitalism and the progress of historical science in the eighteenth century, the world-view of the West had been essentially static, Parmenidean and unhistorical until the advent of romanticism. The most important factors in human culture, the principles of the natural and supernatural world order, the laws of morality and logic, the ideals of truth and right, the destiny of man and the purpose of social institutions, had been regarded as fundamentally unequivocal and immutable in their significance, as timeless entelechies or as innate ideas. In relation to the constancy of these principles, all change, all development and differentiation had appeared irrelevant and ephemeral; everything that occurred in the medium of historical time seemed to touch merely the surface of things. Only from the time of the Revolution and the romantic movement did the nature of man and society begin to appear as essentially evolutionistic and dynamic. The idea that we and our culture are involved in eternal flux and endless struggle, the notion that our intellectual life is a process with a merely transitory character, is a discovery of romanticism and represents its most important contribution to the philosophy of the present age. . . .

Historicism, which was connected with a complete reorientation of culture, was the expression of deep existential changes, and corresponded to an upheaval which shook the very foundations of society. The political revolution had abolished the old barriers between the classes and the economic revolution had intensified the mobility of life to a previously inconceivable degree. Romanticism was the ideology of the new society and the expression of the world-view of a generation which no longer believed in absolute values, could no longer believe in any values without thinking of their relativity, their historical limitations. It saw everything tied to historical suppositions, because it had experienced, as part of its own personal destiny, the downfall of the old and the rise of the new culture. The romantic awareness of the historicity of all social life was so deep that even the conservative classes were able to produce only historical arguments to justify their privileges, and based their claims on seniority and the fact of being firmly rooted in the historical culture of the nation. But the historical world-view was by no means the creation of conservatism, as has repeatedly been asserted; the conservative classes merely appropriated it to themselves and developed it in a special direction and one opposite to its original purpose. The progressive middle class saw in the historical origin of social institutions evidence against their absolute validity, whereas the conservative classes, who, in their endeavour to justify their privileges, had nothing to appeal to but their "historical rights," their age and their priority, gave historicism a new meaning — they disguised the antithesis between historicity and supra-temporal validity, and created in its stead an antagonism between the product of historical growth and steady evolution, on the one hand, and the individual, rational, reformist act of volition, on the other. The antithesis here was not between time and timelessness, history and absolute being, positive law and natural law, but between "organic development" and individual arbitrariness.

History becomes the refuge of all the elements of society at variance with their own age, whose intellectual and material existence is threatened; and the refuge, above all, of the intelligentsia, which now feels disillusioned in its hopes and tricked out of its rights, not only in Germany but also in the countries of Western Europe. The lack of influence on political developments, which had hitherto been the fate of the German intellectuals, now becomes a European-wide fate shared by intellectuals in general. The Enlightenment and the Revolution had encouraged the individual to cherish exorbitant hopes; they had seemed to promise the unrestricted reign of reason and the absolute authority of writers and thinkers. In the eighteenth century, writers were the intellectual leaders of the West; they were the dynamic element behind the reform movement, they embodied the ideal of personality by which the progressive classes were guided. The upshot of the Revolution changed all that. They were now made responsible by turns for the Revolution having done too much and too little, and were in no way able to maintain their prestige in this period of stagnation and mental eclipse. Even when they were in agreement with the prevailing forces of reaction and were serving them faithfully, they felt none of the satisfaction enjoyed by the *"philosophes"* of the eighteenth century. Most of them saw themselves condemned to absolute ineffectiveness and had the feeling of being quite superfluous. They took refuge in a past which they made the place where all their dreams and wishes came true and from which they excluded all the tensions between idea and reality, the self and the world, the individual and society. . . . The feeling of homelessness and loneliness became the fundamental experience of the new generation; their whole outlook on the world was influenced by it. It assumed innumerable forms and found expression in a whole series of attempts to escape, of which turning to the past was merely the most pronounced. The escape to Utopia and the fairy tale, to the unconscious and the fantastic, the uncanny and the mysterious, to childhood and nature, to dreams and madness, were all disguised and more or less sublimated forms of the same feeling, of the same yearning for irresponsibility and a life free from suffering and frustration — all attempts to escape into that chaos and anarchy against which the classicism of the seventeenth and eighteenth centuries had fought at times with alarm and anger, at others with grace and wit, but always with the same determination. The classicist felt himself to be master of reality; he agreed to be ruled by others, because he ruled himself and believed that life can be ruled. The romantic, on the other hand, acknowledged no external ties, was incapable of committing himself, and felt himself to be defencelessly exposed to an overwhelmingly powerful reality; hence his contempt for and simultaneous deification of reality. He either violated it or surrendered himself to it blindly and unresistingly, but he never felt equal to it. . . .

The post-revolutionary period was an age of general disappointment. For those who were only superficially connected with the ideas of the Revolution this disillusion began with the Convention, for the real revolutionaries with the 9 Thermidor. The first group gradually came to hate everything that reminded it of the Revolution, for the latter every new stage in the development only confirmed the treachery of their former confederates. But it was also a painful awakening for those for whom the dream of the Revolution had been a nightmare from the very beginning. To all of them the present age seemed to have become stale and empty. The intellectuals isolated themselves more and more from the rest of society, and the intellectually productive elements already lived a life of their own. The concept of the philistine and the *"bourgeois,"* in contrast to the *"citoyen,"* arose, and the curious and almost unprecedented situation came about that artists and writers were filled with hatred and contempt for the very class to which they owed their intellectual and material existence. For romanticism was essentially a middle-class movement, indeed, it was the middle-class literary school par excellence, the school which had broken for good with the conventions of classicism, courtly-aristocratic rhetoric and pretence, with elevated style and refined language. . . . Romantic art is the first to consist in the "human document," the screaming confession, the open wound laid bare. When the literature of the enlightenment praises the bourgeois, it is always done merely in order to attack the upper classes; the romantic movement is the first to take it for granted that the bourgeois is the measure of man. The fact that so many of the representatives of romanticism were of noble descent no more alters the bourgeois character of the movement than does the anti-philistinism of its cultural policy. Novalis, von Kleist, von Arnim, von Eichendorff and von Chamisso, Viscomte de Chateaubriand, de Lamartine, de Vigny, de Musset, de Bonald, de Maistre and de Lamennais, Lord Byron and Shelley, Leopardi and Manzoni, Pushkin and Lermontov, were members of aristocratic families and manifested aristocratic views to some extent, but from the time of the romantic movement, literature was intended exclusively for the free market, that is to say, for a middle-class public. It was occasionally possible to persuade this public to accept political opinions contrary to its real interests, but it was no longer possible to present the world to it in the impersonal style and abstract intellectual patterns of the eighteenth century. The world-view that was really suited to it was expressed most clearly of all in the idea of the autonomy of the mind and the immanence of the individual spheres of culture, which had predominated in German philosophy since Kant and which would have been unthinkable without the emancipation of the middle class. . . . It was only after the dissolution of the earlier ties, after

the disappearance of the feeling of the absolute nullity of the mind in relation to
the divine order and its relative nullity in
relation to the ecclesiastical and secular
hierarchy, that is, after the individual had
been referred back to himself, that the idea
of intellectual autonomy became conceivable. It was in harmony with the philosophy of economic and political liberalism,
and remained current until socialism created the idea of a new obligation and historical materialism again abolished the
autonomy of the mind. This autonomy was,
therefore, like the individualism of romanticism, the result and not the cause of the
conflict which shook the foundations of
eighteenth-century society. Neither of these
ideas was absolutely new, but this was the
first time that the individual had been in-
cited to revolt against society and against
everything that stood between him and his
happiness.

Romanticism pushed its individualism to
extremes as a compensation for the materialism of the world and as a protection
against the hostility of the bourgeoisie and
the philistines to the things of the mind.
As the pre-romantics had already tried to
do, the romantics proper wanted to create
with their aestheticism a sphere withdrawn
from the rest of the world in which they
could reign unhindered. . . .

The inner strife of the romantic soul is
reflected nowhere so directly and expres-
sively as in the figure of the "second self"
which is always present to the romantic
mind and recurs in innumerable forms and
variations in romantic literature. The source
of this *idée fixe* is unmistakable: it is the
irresistible urge to introspection, the mani-
acal tendency to self-observation and the
compulsion to consider oneself over and
over again as one unknown, as an uncan-
nily remote stranger. The idea of the "second self" is, of course, again merely an
attempt to escape and expresses the inability of the romantics to resign themselves
to their own historical and social situation.
The romantic rushes headlong into his
"double," just as he rushes headlong into

everything dark and ambiguous, chaotic
and ecstatic, demonic and dionysian, and
seeks therein merely a refuge from the reality which he is unable to master by rational
means. On this flight from reality, he discovers the unconscious, that which is hidden away in safety from the rational mind,
the source of his wish-fulfilment dreams
and of the irrational solutions of his problems. He discovers that "two souls dwell
in his breast," that something inside him
feels and thinks that is not identical with
himself, that he carries his demon and his
judge about with him — in brief, he discovers the basic facts of psychoanalysis. For
him, the irrational has the inestimable advantage of not being subject to conscious
control, which is why he praises the unconscious, obscure instincts, dreamlike and ecstatic states of soul, and looks in them for
the satisfaction which is not vouchsafed
him by the cool, cold, critical intellect. . . .
Hence the belief in direct experiences and
moods, the surrender to the moment and
the fleeting impression, hence that adoration of the "chance occurrence" of which
Novalis speaks. The more bewildering the
chaos, the more radiant the star, it is hoped,
that will emerge from it. Hence the cult
of the mysterious and nocturnal, of the bizarre and the grotesque, the horrible and
the ghostlike, the diabolical and the macabre, the pathological and the perverse. . . .

The political conversion of romanticism
in Germany from liberalism to the monarchist-conservative point of view, the opposite trend of development in France and
in England, too, in a probably more complicated way, wavering between Revolution and Restoration, but on the whole in
harmony with the French development,
was possible only because romanticism had
an equivocal relationship to the Revolution
and was at all times ready to change over
to the opposite of its previous attitude. . . .
The revolutionary spirit was always of a
different character in Germany from what
it was in France. The German poets' enthusiasm for the Revolution was abstract and
fact-distorting in its approach and no more

did justice to the meaning of events than the thoughtless tolerance of the ruling classes. The poets thought of the Revolution as a great philosophical discussion, the holders of power regarded it as a mere play that, in their opinion, could never become a reality in Germany. This lack of understanding explains the complete change that comes over the whole nation after the Wars of Liberation. The change of front of Fichte, the republican and rationalist, who suddenly sees the period of the Revolution as the age of "absolute sinfulness," is supremely typical. The initial romanticization of the Revolution only brings about an all the more violent repudiation and results in the identification of romanticism with the Restoration. At the time when the romantic movement reached its really creative and revolutionary phase in the West, there was no longer a single romantic in Germany who had not transferred his allegiance to the conservative and monarchist camp.

French romanticism, which in its beginnings was an "émigré literature," remained the mouthpiece of the Restoration until after 1820. It is only in the second half of the 20's that it develops into a liberal movement formulating its artistic aims after the analogy of the political Revolution. In England romanticism is, as in Germany, prorevolutionary, to begin with, and becomes conservative only during the war against Napoleon; after the war years, however, it takes a fresh turn, and again approaches its earlier revolutionary ideals. Romanticism, therefore, finally turns against the Restoration and reaction both in France and England — and, indeed, much more decidedly than the course of political events themselves. . . .

In France the romantics profess themselves legitimists and clericalists, to begin with, whereas the classical tradition in literature is represented mainly by the liberals. Not all the classicists are liberal, but all the liberals are classicists. . . . In their fight against romanticism, however, the liberal and conservative classicists are in complete agreement; that is why the Academy

rejects Lamartine, despite his conservatism. Incidentally, the Academy no longer represents the taste prevailing among the literary public; a large section of the reading public supports the romantics and, indeed, with a hitherto unknown fervour. . . . To be sure, the reading public is not big, but it is a grateful public with a passionate interest in and enthusiasm for literature. A relatively large number of books is bought, the press follows literary events with the greatest attention, the *salons* open up again and celebrate the intellectual heroes of the day. As a result of the relatively high degree of freedom, a disintegration of literary effort takes place and the homogeneous culture of the "*grand siècle*" gradually recedes into a mythical past. . . .

The amalgamation of the French romantics into a homogeneous group takes place at the same time as public opinion takes a turn to liberalism. . . .

The Bohemian character with which romanticism is usually associated was by no means characteristic of the movement from the outset. From Chateaubriand to Lamartine, French romanticism was represented almost exclusively by aristocrats, and if, after 1824, it no longer stood up unanimously for the monarchy and the Church, nevertheless, it remained to some extent aristocratic and clerical. Only very gradually does the leadership of the movement pass into the hands of the plebeians Victor Hugo, Théophile Gautier, and Alexandre Dumas, and only shortly before the July revolution do the majority of the romantics change their conservative attitude. The emergence into prominence of the plebeian elements is, however, more a symptom than the cause of the political change. Formerly the middle-class writers adapted themselves to the conservatism of the aristocrats, whereas now even the aristocratic Chateaubriand and Lamartine go over to the opposition. The ever-advancing restriction of personal freedom under Charles X, the clericalization of public life, the introduction of the death penalty for blasphemy, the dissolution of the Garde Nationale and the

Chamber, government by decree, only accelerate the radicalization of intellectual life. They only make more obvious what had already been unmistakable since 1815, namely that the Restoration meant the definitive end of the Revolution. Men's minds have now at last recovered from their post-revolutionary apathy and it was this change of mood which forced Charles X to take more and more reactionary measures, if he wanted to keep to the direction imperative for a government based on anti-revolutionary elements. The romantics, who gradually became conscious of where the Restoration was really leading to, recognized at the same time that the wealthy bourgeoisie was the strongest support of the régime — a much stronger support than the old, partly dispossessed, disabled aristocracy. Their whole hatred, their whole contempt, was now heaped on the middle class. The avaricious, narrow-minded, hypocritical bourgeois became their public enemy No. 1 and, in contrast to him, the poor, honest, open-hearted artist struggling against all the humiliating ties and conventional lies of society appears as the human ideal par excellence. The tendency to remoteness from practical life with firm social roots and political commitments, which had been characteristic of romanticism from the very beginning and had become apparent in Germany even in the eighteenth century, now becomes predominant everywhere; even in the Western nations an unbridgeable gulf opens up between the genius and ordinary men, between the artist and the public, between art and social reality. The bad manners and impertinences of the bohemians, their often childish ambition to embarrass and provoke the unsuspecting bourgeois, their frantic attempt to differentiate themselves from normal, average men and women, the eccentricity of their clothes, their headdress, their beards, Gautier's red waistcoat and the equally conspicuous, though not always so dazzling masquerade of his friends, their free and easy and paradoxical language, their exaggerated, aggressively formulated ideas, their invectives and indecencies, all that is merely the expression of the desire to isolate themselves from the middle-class society, or rather of the desire to represent the already accomplished isolation as intentional and acceptable.

With the *Jeune-France,* as the rebels now call themselves, everything revolves around their hatred for philistinism, around their contempt for the strictly regulated and soulless life of the bourgeoisie, around their fight against everything traditional and conventional, everything capable of being taught and learnt, everything mature and serene. The system of intellectual values is enriched by a new category: the idea of youth as more creative than and intrinsically superior to age. . . .

The most important achievement of the romantic revolution was the renewal of the poetic vocabulary. The French literary language had become poor and colourless in the course of the seventeenth and eighteenth century, owing to the strict convention regarding permissible expressions and stylistic forms recognized as "correct." Everything that sounded commonplace, professional, archaic, or provincial was taboo. The simple, natural expressions used in everyday language had to be replaced with noble, choice, "poetic" terms or artistic paraphrases. . . . The advocates of the classical style knew quite well, however, what the fundamental issue was. Victor Hugo's language was really nothing new; it was, in fact, the language of the boulevard theatres. But the classicists were merely concerned with the "purity" of the literary theatre; they did not bother themselves about the boulevards and the entertainment of the masses. So long as an elevated theatre and cultivated writing existed, it was possible confidently to disregard what was happening on the boulevards, but once it was permitted to speak from the stage of the Théâtre-Français as one chose, then there was no longer any recognizable difference between the various cultural and social strata. . . .

. . . English romanticism developed

more continuously, more consistently and met with less public resistance than French romanticism; its political evolution was also more homogeneous than the corresponding movement in France. To begin with, it was absolutely liberal and thoroughly well disposed towards the Revolution; it was only the war against Napoleon which led to an understanding between the romantics and the conservative elements and only after his fall that liberalism became predominant in romantic literature once again. . . . English romanticism had its origins essentially in the reaction of the liberal elements to the Industrial Revolution, whereas French romanticism arose from the reaction of the conservative classes to the political revolution. . . . In England the same relation existed between romanticism and the successful completion of the Industrial Revolution as between pre-romanticism and the preparatory stages of the industrialization of society. Goldsmith's *Deserted Village*, Blake's "Satanic Mills" and Shelley's "Age of Despair" are all the expression of an essentially identical mood. The romantics' enthusiasm for nature is just as unthinkable without the isolation of the town from the countryside as is their pessimism without the bleakness and misery of the industrial cities. They realize perfectly what is going on and are acutely aware of the significance of the transformation of human labour into a mere commodity. Southey and Coleridge see in periodical unemployment the necessary consequence of uncontrolled capitalist production and Coleridge already stresses the fact that, in accordance with the new conception of work, the employer buys and the employee sells something that neither of them has the right to buy or sell, namely "the labourer's health, life and well-being."

After the end of the struggle against Napoleon, England finds herself, if in no sense exhausted, at least weakened and intellectually bewildered — in a condition especially calculated to make the middle class aware of the problematical bases of its existence. The younger romantics, the generation of Shelley, Keats, and Byron, are the leading influences in this process. Their uncompromising humanism is their protest against the policy of exploitation and oppression; their unconventional way of life, their aggressive atheism and their lack of moral bias are the different modes of their struggle against the class that controls the means of exploitation and suppression. . . .

. . . The anti-revolutionary hysteria has poisoned the intellectual atmosphere in which the English writers of the eighteenth century had freely developed their abilities; the intellectual manifestations of the period take on an unreal, world-shunning and world-denying character which was absolutely alien to earlier English literature. The most gifted poets of Shelley's generation are not appreciated by the public; they feel homeless and they take refuge abroad. This generation is doomed in England as well as in Germany or Russia; Shelley and Keats are worried to death by their age just as mercilessly as Hoelderlin and Kleist or Pushkin and Lermontov. Ideologically, too, the result is the same everywhere: idealism in Germany, "*l'art pour l'art*" in France, aestheticism in England. Everywhere the struggle ends with a turning away from reality and the abandonment of any effort to change the structure of society. . . .

Byron was the first English poet to play a leading role in European literature, Walter Scott the second. Through them what Goethe understood by "world literature" became a full reality. Their school embraced the whole literary world, enjoyed the highest authority, introduced new forms, new values, set intellectual traffic flowing backwards and forwards between the countries of Europe, carrying along with it new talents and often raising them above their masters. One only needs to think of Pushkin and Balzac to realize the extent and the importance of this school. The vogue of Byron was perhaps more feverish and more obtrusive, but the influence of Walter Scott, who has been described as the "most successful writer in the world," was more solid and more profound. It was his work that inspired the revival of the naturalistic novel, the modern literary genre par excellence, and thereby led to the transformation of the whole modern reading public. The number of readers had been rising steadily in England since the beginning of the eighteenth century. One can distinguish three stages in this process of growth: the phase that begins around 1710 with the new periodicals and culminates in the novels of the middle of the century; the period of the pseudo-historical thriller from 1770 to roughly 1800; and the period of the modern romantic-naturalistic novel that begins with Walter Scott. Each of these periods produced a considerable increase in the reading public. In the first, only a comparatively small section of the middle class was enlisted for secular belles-lettres, people who up till then had never read books at all or at best the products of devotional literature; in the second, this public was enlarged by wide sections of the increasingly wealthy bourgeoisie, mostly women; in the third, elements belonging partly to the higher, partly to the lower strata of the middle class, looking for entertainment as well as instruction in the novel, were added. . . . Walter Scott succeeded in achieving the popularity of the thriller by the more fastidious methods of the great novelists of the eighteenth century. He popularized the portrayal of the feudal past that had hitherto been exclusively the reading of the upper classes, and, at the same time, raised the pseudo-historical shocker to a really literary level.

Responses to Revolution

EDWIN BERRY BURGUM

Edwin Berry Burgum has taught literature at New York University and
has published two volumes of literary criticism. He, like Hauser, is concerned
to distinguish the social roots of Romanticism, but he employs his distinctions
among German, English, and French responses to revolution for the purpose of
definition as well as that of explanation of Romanticism.

H E who seeks to define Romanticism
is entering a hazardous occupation
which has claimed many victims. It would
be foolhardy to desire to multiply the difficulties. I wish to state at the outset, therefore, that I am not concerned with that
Romanticism which is taken for the eternal opposite to the principle of Classicism.
The thesis that literary expression oscillates
between the two contradictory limits of
Romanticism and Classicism, in much the
same way as the human society or the conduct of the individual may be presumed
to oscillate between the two opposite poles
of Good and Evil, is an intriguing point
of view that will have to be left to another
occasion. For the present, I am content
with the more limited problem of defining
the Romanticism of what is generally called
the Romantic Period in European Literature, that century which may be roughly
described as stretching for fifty years on
either side of the year 1800.

Certainly a comprehensive definition of
this Romanticism, with some sharpness to
it, is desirable. For in the past our comprehensive definitions have not been sharp,
and our sharp ones have been provincial.
The general definition generally agreed
upon is that Romanticism comprises the
myriad escapes from Neoclassicism. Unless
Romantic literature is much less significant
than has been habitually assumed, such a

negative statement only conceals the bank-
ruptcy of the effort. The sharp definitions,
on the other hand, by appearing to contra-
dict one another, prove their inadequacy.
Brunetière, for instance, called Romanticism the discovery of the ego. Others have
said that it was the discovery of nature;
still others, the return to medievalism.
Watts-Dunton believed it the rediscovery
of wonder, and an American clergyman-
critic of the transcendental period praised it
as the literature of aspiration. More recently, Professor Babbitt has been disgusted
by its approval of the irrational; Mario Praz
accuses it of having been the hotbed of decadence; whereas critics of sociological interest deplore its stimulus to escape from
reality. We need not become alarmed if
differences in critical standards lurk among
these variations of descriptive effort. The
descriptions are all correct when applied to
individual authors. Byron and Hugo are
clearly egoistic. Chateaubriand and Wordsworth are absorbed by description of the
scenery. Scott in England and Tieck in
Germany represent a medieval revival. But
there is aspiration, the hope for a better
world, in Shelley and in Hugo also, while
in the later work of Chateaubriand and
Shelley many persons have found an escape from reality into a world beyond our
time and space.

When certain tendencies are recognized,

From "Romanticism," by E. B. Burgum in *Kenyon Review*, Vol. III, no. 4 (Autumn, 1941), pp.
479–490. By permission of the *Kenyon Review*.

however, this apparent disorder can be reduced. If medievalism be extended to include the earlier period of the dark ages, to include the nonclassical past generally, and indeed the orient and the classical past itself interpreted nonclassically, then "medievalism" becomes the earliest tendency, which survived chiefly in Germany, to a certain extent in England, and, except for the romances of Dumas, hardly at all in France. Furthermore, it is important to note that, of all the manifestations of Romanticism, this was the most nebulous in content and the most remote from practical concerns. It assumed that the values of heroism, adventure, freedom of the ideal in a word, existed in almost any type of society that was not in the tradition of classicism, that was neither one's own society nor that of the immediately preceding neoclassical period.

As for the second tendency, which would make Romanticism stress individualism, the expansion of the ego, though it was generally characteristic in a variety of relationships to what we have called the early "medievalism," continental writers, like Brandes, for the most part consider it an adequate definition, and equate Romanticism with Byronism. But Byronism faded away in Germany after the early robber literature, remained a minor current in England, and flourished only in France. Byron was forced to flee his native England, and such Byronism as remained was transformed into the personalities of Carlyle and Tennyson. Byronism, however, was the very mark of French Romanticism, as represented in literature by Rousseau and later by Hugo, and in everyday life by the tradition of Rousseau as sharpened into the image of Napoleon.

In England, on the contrary, if we accept Arnold's verdict, the naturism of Wordsworth was the central stream. The interest in nature and country life had been a literary influence in England long before Wordsworth. After the Elizabethan period, it arrogates attention in a mixture of observation, fantasy, and mysticism, in the work of such poets as Traherne. It persists even in Pope to mark the limitations upon the acceptance of Neoclassicism in England, and at the breakdown of the reputation of Pope, it surges into a position of dominance. West, Akenside, Shenstone, Thomson, Crabbe, Cowper, Gray, the graveyard, the English garden, the country village all give evidence that the urban centralizing tendency of Neoclassicism had continually been resisted in England. Later, it infects Scott; it is present in Coleridge, and Keats's poetry only emphasizes its aesthetic side. Every English Romanticist, whatever else he is, is also a poet of nature. But the important feature of English nature poetry is that, save in Byron, it is not Byronic. To Wordsworth, nature is an objective reality, virtually synonymous with God, to which the poet reverently subordinates himself. It is a discipline imposed upon individualism rather than an encouragement to the expanding ego. Wordsworth merely returns to and transforms the English naturism of the Seventeenth Century.

We have, then, achieved at least a partial order in discovering that these three different definitions of Romanticism predominated in three different countries: medievalism in Germany, individualism in France, and naturism in England. In taking the next step, to bring the three together into one, we must pay our respect to another generally accepted statement about Romanticism. We are willing to agree with Professor Babbitt's assertion that the immediate ideological stimulus to international Romanticism was the writing of Rousseau. During the French Revolution, Rousseau's ideas were conveniently compressed into the symbolic form of the well-known slogan: liberté, égalité, fraternité. These three terms obviously do not correspond to the three we have previously used. They isolate one aspect of Romanticism, the political; but it was the most important aspect in contemporary opinion, and we should expect it to furnish the clue to our definition.

The implications of the phrase, liberty,

fraternity, equality, appear, it must be recognized, in uncrystallized form throughout early Romantic literature. The phrase itself, in fact, is merely the sharp antithesis to neoclassical principles: liberty is the opposite to the classical submission of the individual to the eternal order of the universe; equality, a denial of the aristocratic hierarchy of social classes and abstract values; and fraternity, a rejection of feudal disdain for democracy and the common man. The early robber literature, though deficient as successful aesthetic expression, has immense historical importance since, by inference and negatively, it anticipates the conscious and positive statement of aims in the lay trinity of the French Revolution. If the attainment of the slogan represents a revolt against Neoclassicism, it attempts, on the positive side, to define a democracy to take its place. But the aspect of revolt, despite the positive nature of the slogan, remained in one form or another the more immediately attractive. It remained easier to define men's objections to the past than their hopes for the future.

We are ready, then, to accept the historic fact of the French Revolution in the way in which it has usually been accepted, as extremely important for our definition. But this fact, again, is useful to the literary historian only in a negative way. It can hardly explain why, for instance, if the English reject the slogan, they promote instead the naturism of Wordsworth. To reach this positive explanation, we must go behind the French Revolution itself, and investigate the socio-economic changes of which it was only the most startling and belated expression. Only then does it become clear why the trinity of liberty, equality, fraternity, into which the general European spirit of revolt crystallized, was premature for Germany, essential for France, and dangerous for England; and was therefore neglected and discarded in Germany, extolled in France, and both opposed and discarded in England. The literary distinctions we have been making correspond to national distinctions in historical development. They relate to the progress of commercial expansion with the aid of the industrial revolution, and to the socio-political dominance of the middle class that accompanied it. We shall define Romanticism as the cultural manifestation of these material changes. The fact that there was no industrial revolution in Germany but a persistence of feudalism until the unification late in the Nineteenth Century explains both the unrealistic excess of revolt in early German Romantic literature, like Schiller's *Robbers,* and its later dissipation into the vague fantastic world of a vanished medievalism. But more important for our immediate purpose is the fact that the industrial revolution came first to England and proceeded there with such a minimum of shock that the word "revolution" seems quite out of place.

In fact we must go back still further, and recognize that the important revolution in England, the "great revolution of 1688," came after the civil wars of the mid-Seventeenth Century; and that it, too, was accomplished with a minimum of bloodshed and disorder. The prevailing psychological tone of English literature and of the English personality since the days of Elizabeth reflects a stabilization of the more robust impetuosity of the Renaissance under the smooth and rapid evolution of her commercial ascendancy. . . . When the French Revolution broke, however, the now openly dominant English middle class, suddenly faced with a foreign hazard, unconsciously reacted to the emerging native hazard also. They embraced Methodism, and, under the broader name of evangelicalism, transformed it from a spontaneous popular desire for self-improvement into a sanctification of sacrifice and hard labor. The transformation of pre-Romanticism into the full-blown Romantic movement of Wordsworth and Shelley is the consequence of these reactions in more mundane spheres. Romanticism, which had previously been a confusion of anti-classical tendencies, now becomes a movement for the stabilization of English society along lines that have already been set.

Once more it must be noted that the English pre-Romantic literature, though influenced by the international movement, had always recoiled from the radicalism of its continental expression. There had never been, since the medieval Robin Hood ballads, any English literature sympathetic toward robbers and outcasts. . . . Pre- Romanticism, it is true, brings a change of literary theme. The common man becomes the object of attention. But, save in one scene, Thomson finds no reason for pitying the farmer and he certainly does not inflate him into heroic proportions; he is content to describe with quiet reserve the satisfactions of country life. There is no more bitterness of revolt in *The Seasons* than in Whittier's *Snowbound*. When the common man becomes the object of sympathy, as in Gray's "Elegy," the poet to our surprise states with prophetic melancholy that the poor man's rights and hopes are doomed to disappointment. English pre-Romantic poetry is gloomy with premonition of impending change in a world of unexpected hazards.

Strangely enough, it might seem, the optimistic view is largely a phenomenon of the literature after the French Revolution. When Englishmen grew really frightened, their literature leaped to provide a more therapeutic tone. It now ignores the more specific topics of its melancholy concern. It lifts its eyes from the miseries of the poor. It abandons its growing consciousness of class distinctions, and sees a general improvement in store for everybody. It takes a cosmic view of progress, starting, let us say, with Erasmus Darwin and culminating within our period in the prose of Godwin and the early poetry of Shelley. But progress, however cosmic, looked too much like revolt. It dropped out of the picture with the reputation of Godwin, only to arise once more in the less excitable metaphors of the Victorian period. Contemplation of nature proved less vertiginous, and Shelley, who could not achieve the requisite calm,

could at least, in Arnold's phrase, turn to chasing rainbows. The industrial class, shuddering at the mention of the French Revolution, disliked even the verbalization of the progress their own machines were making, and wished only to be left in peace to run them.

The situation in England, then, was the opposite to that in France. And the difference between the two literatures flows from this fact, the difference between a literature of nature and one celebrating liberty, fraternity, equality. The political revolution that swept away the feudalism of the French monarchy was a belated result of the same pressures which had extorted the Bill of Rights from the monarch a century before in England. But the timing makes an enormous difference in these matters; it is always new water that passes under the old bridge of general statement. In a France which must overtake an already industrialized England, not only was the change more abrupt, but it could not take place without the active cooperation of the lower classes and without their consciously expecting to share its benefits. Hence a more inclusive watchword than the liberty of free worship of the English Civil Wars was necessary. In liberty, fraternity, equality was symbolized the fact that the proletariat felt itself on a par with the bourgeoisie in the establishment of parliamentary forms and national prosperity; and the bourgeoisie, by accepting this battle-cry, revealed its need for the voluntary support of the masses. The English mercantile class a century earlier could compromise with its feudal enemy on nonessential issues. But the starved French bourgeoisie was forced to compromise with its proletarian ally on the essential. If the Terror was a reflection of the tendency of the Revolution to go beyond bourgeois needs and transfer power to even poorer classes, the reaction to it put the new commercial element firmly in control. The rise of Napoleon was not so much the evidence of a bourgeois excess in the direction of despotism as it was a countenancing of the dissipation of the energy of the masses even at the price of economic advance. This stage is analogous in opposite fashion to the English compromise of the Restoration. The English had fooled the aristocracy by leaving them cultural prestige but only the shadow of actual power. The French now proceeded to distract the masses and the masses proceeded to deceive themselves through the prestige of Napoleon. The little corporal who became an emperor not only killed off in his wars the necessary number of those who were clamoring for fraternity and equality; he sought to establish a new interpretation of the whole trinity. Fraternity and equality now expressed themselves through cooperative submission to the liberty of the great man who has once been small; the only liberty the soldier asks is to obey his command heroically. But Napoleon's slogans failed with his practical failure, and shattered the trinity into the countless gleaming fragments of individualism, as Brunetière has said. The memory of Napoleon sets up extreme variations of aggressive competitive egoism which quite swallow (in the love life, for example, if not in the novels of George Sand) the older celebration of fraternity and equality. But an historic fact can never be completely erased, so long as the social compulsions which engendered it persist. Buildings continued to bear the once magnetic words of revolutionary days. The needs of the proletariat could not be entirely neglected, and the slogan of cooperation remained to clarify more widely among the French than in any other country the existence of competition among the classes.

The unconscious aim of English Romanticism, on the other hand, had been a guarantee that this demoralizing slogan never got into English circulation. It had not been needed at the earlier period when the English middle classes established themselves without any conspicuous need for the avowed cooperation of the lower classes, which still obeyed their betters without much question. Therefore, the dominant class saw no reason now to import from abroad an embarrassment to its power. It remained quite satisfied with the statement of Burke. Hence the somersaults of the Romantics from their earlier hopeful reflection of the French Revolution into whatever variety of contradictory doctrine seemed, by guaranteeing their individualism, still to guarantee their individual integrity. The later Wordsworth, Southey, Shelley, Coleridge, however different, are all alike in their silence on the themes of fraternity and equality and in their eloquence in inflating liberty into a harmless impractical ambiguity. Only Byron remained conscious of the dilemma, which tormented him in "The Isles of Greece," where he had fled the moral censure of his countrymen. In Wordsworth, the most candid of the lot, the word is virtually discarded. Peasants, like nuns, fret not within their freeholds, or so he said; and set a good example to the disgruntled townspeople.

At the same time, one should not picture the middle classes of the period in colors too similar to the villains of nineteenth-century melodrama. They were industrious men who honestly believed that the prosperity of the country was knit up with their own. They were the victims of their own ambiguities, and felt, as Carlyle demanded, that they were clothing the backs of all mankind as well as amassing the fortunes their energies deserved. They shared the cheering belief in progress, and if they confused their own progress with that of mankind, it was that they assumed as firmly as any aristocracy the existence of permanent limitations to the legitimate demands of the masses of men. Competition applied to the individual and not to the class, if indeed it was not limited to individuals within the middle classes, and all working-class resistance to the employer was in their eyes simply wrong and unprogressive. The differing slogans of the Romantic movement, whether in France or in England, were therefore completely sincere, however practically misleading. Since they worked within bourgeois ranks, they were taken for universals. But they were working at the same time, though in opposite ways, within the ranks of the laboring classes in both countries. The English conception of liberty as the orderly life of the peasant under the oak tree permitted the ambiguity to become hopelessly confusing, after the defeat of Chartism, under the increased stresses of the Victorian period. But the more comprehensive French trinity had been imbedded in the imagination of the French working class: so that, later on, when the intellectuals decided it was delusive, the lower classes were beginning to define its validity with greater particularity. The cynicism of Flaubert, the perversity of Baudelaire, in general the pessimistic strain that dominated the best French literature as the nineteenth century grew older, represents the bourgeois rejection of its old slogan; whereas the optimistic conclusion to Zola's *Germinal* shows a friend of the working class accepting as true the very slogan which the class that originated it was in process of discarding as error. But in England Tennyson, who continues the English tradition of liberty in nature, and the Romantic quest for a universal that transcends the limitations of class, can only flounder in abstractions like his faint trust in the larger hope and the higher pantheism. And poetry loses the sharp images, the meaty nut of meaning to crack, that

Shakespeare and even Wordsworth in his fashion could once attain.

Naturally in such a sketch I have no time to distinguish interesting variations on these themes in individual writers. Nor can I relate these social influences to marked changes in literary techniques. But it must be added, as a necessary aesthetic generalization which I have by inference employed, that these social influences have seldom been directly reflected in literature. What art directly reflects is the actual psychological organization of men as it shows itself in daily life. It reflects economic influences only as these have transformed styles in ideas and practice of living. It gives the results, and leaves the causes pretty much to be inferred. Hence the economic causes appear in literature only as they have been changed or distorted into the discrepancy that has always existed between the real motives of men's actions and men's consciousness of these motives. Romantic literature, in particular, is interesting because antagonisms between the middle and lower classes which could not be frankly faced led to such startling perversions in the literary expression of these basic causes as we have analyzed. But I do not know what other means of definition than these social causes I have used can bring a similar consistency into the definition of Romantic literature.

Romanticism and Industrial Society

ALBERT JOSEPH GEORGE

Albert Joseph George is Professor of Romance Languages at Syracuse University. His study, *The Development of French Romanticism,* is a pioneering effort to trace the interconnections between Romanticism and the progress of the industrial revolution in France. With a narrower focus and more detailed examination he pursues some of the general concerns expressed by Hauser and Burgum.

INTRODUCTION

The study of French romanticism has provided scholars with one of the most entertaining and irritating of literary puzzles. For generations they have vainly tried to reduce a complex series of disparate elements to a brief but satisfactory definition. Periodically one writer or another has blackened hundreds of pages in attempts to find a phrase which might function as mental calipers for measuring the exact degree of a writer's romanticism. Whenever such a definition has been proposed, critics have cheerfully listed sins of omission, tearing down carefully-prepared arguments or offering substitute interpretations. But still other optimists have always risen to the challenge, sure that they could solve the riddle — and so goes the game.

Scholars being among the most contrary of men, the net result has been a wealth of contradictory statements. And the situation has not been improved by the fact that historically the romanticists themselves were not sure how to explain their work. . . . From the well-known "libéralisme en littérature" of Hugo, to the famous quip of Stendhal on the modernity of romanticism, the writers varied in interpreting their own ideas. Consequently, it is no wonder that the Baron Seillière saw in romanticism a kind of naturistic mysticism, while Auguste Viatte traced it back to the occult and illuministic philosophies of the 18th century. On the other hand, a chauvinistic Louis Reynaud considered it the result of the evil influence of foreign cultures, although Pierre Moreau understood it as a vast reaching for the infinite and a concern for the relative. Irving Babbitt sneered at romanticism as an undue insistence on individualism, but Roger Picard has found it to be a main source of socialism. . . . More recently, Adrien de Meeüs simplified the problem by calling "romantic" everything in man which is opposed to reason, that which seeps from the mysterious and secret corners of the soul.

Contemporary usage of the word presents further difficulties. Romanticism and romanticism exist side by side, with entirely different meanings. For some, romanticism denotes a state of mind that may be contrasted with the precise, regulated symmetry of classicism. Therefore, it is legitimate for them to write on the romanticism of the *Chanson de Roland,* of Pascal, or Voltaire. On the other hand, Romanticism signifies to most people a definite period of history during which specific writers accepted the name to differentiate their particular kind of literature from all others.

From *The Development of French Romanticism, The Impact of the Industrial Revolution on Literature* by Albert Joseph George (Syracuse, 1955), pp. ix–xii, 189–193. By permission of the Syracuse University Press.

It is in this sense that the word is used herein, though without benefit of capitalization.

II

This book does not contain the solution of a problem that has so long perplexed so many. Its intent is simply to introduce a new factor for consideration as an important determinant in the devolpment of romanticism: the Industrial Revolution. The impact of mechanization and the shift to industrial capitalism are phenomena which have been greatly neglected as influences on literature, although they have been universally acknowledged as major creators of social change. The machine, the growth of the urban proletariat and the social consequences of the factory system have, in general, been overlooked in favor of problems of aesthetics. . . .

The fundamental thesis here is that the Industrial Revolution functioned as one of the prime sources of romanticism, and, simultaneously, became a principal force in transforming the initial character of that literature. Replies are sought to such questions as: why did romanticism change so fundamentally about 1830; why did it break into splinter movements; and why these particular movements? Some of the answers can be found by studying both the effect of the Industrial Revolution on society and its influence on the political and literary philosophies of the writers of the period.

III

In this work romanticism has been treated as a phenomenon covering roughly the period 1800–1852, to give it the greatest latitude. To be sure, the historical view of romanticism entails close consideration of an age that saw a fantastic succession of governments, religious cults, economic saviors, and dabblers in the delights of ecstatic mysticism. The various short-lived regimes of the Revolution made way for the Consulate, the Empire, and the Restoration, which in turn culminated in the Orléans Monarchy and the Second Re-

public. During this era, Saint-Simonism and Fourierism vied with the New Jerusalem; Enfantin paraded in splendid costume while his followers were seeking the *femme-messie* in the East; Pierre Leroux and Jean Reynaud disagreed sharply on the interplanetary migration of souls. Simultaneously, a Catholicism outlawed during the Revolution blossomed in rich renascence and writers like Ballanche and Lamartine stirred uneasily, conscious of the way time erodes all institutions. French authors finally rejected most of the tired tenets of the classical aesthetics, while modern history struggled for attention against a popular taste for Gothicism. The age seems one of incredible complexity, with little or no continuity.

One fact, however, does stand out amidst all the chaos. France, blocked from the Industrial Revolution by a great political revolt, the Imperial wars, and the apathy of the Bourbons, suddenly began to feel the shock of industrialization, at about the time when the French romanticists were winning their argument with the neo-classicists.

The effects of the Industrial Revolution were not long in appearing. Romanticism prior to 1830 had been mostly negative in nature, concerned primarily with refuting the claims of classical dicta. By 1830 its supporters had made their point but their very victory created for them the problem of establishing a positive creed if they hoped to keep the attention of the public. And it was the Industrial Revolution which, in part, furnished the new school with the materials it was seeking; new plots, new characters, new images, even a new purpose for writing, came from this great age of major social change.

Not only did the Industrial Revolution yield the reasons and means for revising the content of literature, it also contributed to the establishment of new approaches to art. Writers who, for the first time, faced a mass audience without benefit of patrons, and who were forced to please potential buyers, necessarily had to modify techniques established for communication with an elite. The novel in particular felt this transformation. Hitherto an unimportant genre, it rapidly came to dominate the literary scene and, where once few had given heed to its form, the art of the prose narrative began more and more to concern the majority of writers. Furthermore, authors increasingly felt the need for a new set of symbols and myths to synthesize the beliefs and aspirations of their age, as they attempted to express the feelings of contemporary society. They set to work to fill this gap and, by 1840, romanticism had created a new mythology of its own, a handy frame of reference for the problems of the period.

This, then, is the general thesis. But one word of warning. It should not be assumed that the Industrial Revolution was the only factor governing the development of romanticism, nor that it regulated the growth of the new literature according to a kind of determinism. It should be clearly kept in mind that the events which conspired to push romanticism in the direction it took occurred from historical coincidence. And although 1830 seems to be a magic year, a division line in the development of French literature of the 19th century, it should be remembered that the date is here used primarily as a handy reference and should actually be read as "about 1830." In any case, the concurrence at that time of the phenomena under discussion cannot in any way be attributed to inexorable cause and effect. Chance played the strongest part in the turn of events. . . .

CONCLUSION

Romanticism, it seems, can be divided into at least two distinct periods, with the division coming roughly about 1830. Prior to then, the movement was apparently held together by a negative attitude, by what the young men objected to, not what they stood for. During all the years of the early debate with the classicists, the proponents of the modern had somehow failed to present a manifesto acceptable to all the literary rebels. Thus, while they objected to perpetuating mummified themes, they came to few conclusions on firm proposals for what might fill the void their reaction had created.

Consequently, at first they wisely took Madame de Staël's advice and from their neighbors enthusiastically borrowed plots, themes and symbols, or invoked the magic names of foreign masters to bolster a position weak in the prestige of ancestry. However, progressively as they won their argument for the right to create as they deemed fit, they felt less and less need for foreign aid and, by 1830, they had learned the lessons other nations could teach and belatedly turned their gaze back to France. But all this time, the romanticists had given careful attention only to poetry and the theater. Prose, particularly the novel, had not yet earned their approval, though many of them had dabbled sporadically in this medium.

By 1830, then, the romanticists had freed themselves from restraints but, unbeknownst to them, they were about to be plunged into a strange new world, one far less comfortable than the bumbling and slow-moving Restoration. The industrial Revolution had crossed the Channel in the wake of Wellington; and by the time Louis-Philippe came to power, industrial capitalism was much in evidence. The sudden, even explosive entry of the machine, with all its social consequences, struck the nation just as the romanticists were seeking material to continue their revolution.

Coincidentally, the position of the professional author changed drastically. For the first time writers had the means to reach a mass audience with inexpensive literature. By virtue of the technological advances in printing which it brought, the Industrial Revolution gave them the possibility of a more profitable living than ever, provided they could satisfy the public. Meanwhile, too, this public had been experiencing the effects of the first attempts to introduce mass education in France, experiments which broadened tremendously the potential reading audience. And given the contemporary crisis in the book trade, authors did not have to be told where lay the butter for their bread.

Perhaps to their sorrow, the modernists soon discovered how radically the public had changed, even since the first skirmishes over romanticism. The age belonged to the bourgeoisie, but writers concerned with large editions had also to calculate on the tastes of the peasant and the proletariat, the latter a strange new class that seemed to spring from the sowing of cogwheels. The urban workers did not at first weigh too heavily in the literary balance, though they later would, but from the start they attracted attention because in the conditions of their existence could be seen the violent social effects of the Industrial Revolution and the difficulties the nation faced in adjusting to them. This class and its problems would furnish the young writers with much of the material they used after 1830.

This, then, was the new public. Its low literacy and incapacity for the subtler forms of writing, particularly for any demanding sophistication of taste, had lowered the standards set by the elite of the 17th and 18th centuries. The spread of elementary schooling had made France, not just Paris, the audience to be faced. And this audience had wants far different from those of its intellectual leaders. The upper bourgeoisie might still be classically minded by taste or hostility to change, but the rest of the nation, including both the peasants and the industrial workers, belonged completely to the present. Their outlook was far more practical, since they could not afford to live vicariously in other times, no matter how intriguing the past; and only prose, not poetry, enticed them to spend their hard-earned sous, for this they could grasp as the medium of storytelling.

None but the dullest could escape the fact that the day of prose had come, even though critics still considered it an illegitimate child of the muses. About 1830 poetry had slid into a decline despite the vociferous mourning of its practitioners, immediately to be replaced in the public favor by prose. Publishers shed a delicate tear but no longer considered its existence justified because it did not sell. Economics had conquered the Alexandrine and no respectable professional writer missed the signs pointing to prose.

Just as these facts became obvious, the modern newspaper rose full-formed from the fertile brain of Emile de Girardin. This, too, had been made possible by the Industrial Revolution and it was to have a major effect on literature. In their mad race for subscribers, editors conscious of the habit-forming effects of the feuilleton enticed novelists to their aid. Since the alliance proved profitable to both parties, it tended to become permanent, but it meant that the feuilletoniste, even more than the independent writer, had to submit himself almost completely to the domination of a public given to sudden whimsical shifts in taste. The average man became the arbiter of literary success.

As the preceding series of facts dawned on the romanticists, their revolution changed sharply, almost abruptly. The movement split into factions as its proponents reacted to contemporary events, and literature developed along lines unperceived and undreamed by the men of the Restoration. One segment, dedicated to art for art's sake, rejected the machine and all it represented. These men, a second generation of romanticists, created the myth of the modern avant-garde poet. Leftist in politics, hostile to "bourgeois" values, they continued the experimentation implicit in the preface of *Cromwell* to produce the prose poem and rare and exotic verse forms. But they paid the price in full: their work tended to become increasingly obscure to the layman, with the result that they divorced themselves almost completely from the public as different coteries battled over fine points of prosody.

The other group, the "utilitarians," decided to face contemporary civilization, its factories, slums, and the social problems that followed the advent of an urban proletariat. As self-appointed Messiahs, putative politicians and leaders in a dozen different faiths, they expected to direct the course of their age. Consequently, they sponsored a worker's literature as one of the responsibilities of their position. To their amazement, they found that though some of their protégés meekly repeated advice on accepting one's lot to store up treasures in heaven, others wanted heaven on earth. From the latter would come the rumblings of dissent that presaged the first signs of a socialist literature.

Unlike their younger colleagues, these utilitarians accepted grudgingly the prose which the age craved, particularly the old and hoary romance. But new conditions made some of them consider the medium in which they were working and out of this meditation men like Balzac or Stendhal would see the basis of a new art form, the modern novel. Historically-minded, they would change the romance's point of narration, drop story into the present, and make the analysis of psychologically motivated characters their chief concern. How society made people act on each other interested them more than plots built of incidents strung haphazardly in bead-fashion.

But the novel gave the old romance little competition; the latter flourished in sturdy fashion when the penny press adopted it in the form of a feuilleton designed to attract subscribers. Professional writers, very much business men now that the patron had disappeared, reduced the romance to a recipe for easy serialization. The resultant concoction of stock characters, conventional situations, weary plots, and conversational clichés may have disgusted aesthetes, but the great mass of new readers loved it. And since the latter constituted the source of a writer's bread

and butter, artists accepted the mésalliance of romance and newspaper as a fact of life. Critics might howl at the literary changes, but their position merely forced them into a different kind of art for art's sake. They, like the Petit Cénacle, wrote more and more for an elite, and their former glory fell to a new breed, the reviewer.

Both victors and vanquished, however, seemed to react similarly in one way to the nascent machine age. All felt the need for a more expressive language, an imagery closer to reality and presentational forms tailored for modern conditions. Each in his own way helped rejuvenate in this manner the literature of the nineteenth century. To be sure, they were still adjusting to the effects of the Industrial Revolution but what they did was in some ways a forecast of things to come. In this respect, perhaps, the change in society left its deepest mark.

That the course of Industrial Revolution and the development of romanticism in France are contiguous is beyond question, and, likewise, the fact that they are inextricably intertwined and specifically related is beyond doubt. Yet, to demonstrate a determinism or a causality in any direction, however enticing, would lead beyond the safety of the facts. Nevertheless, it is possible to conclude that the Industrial Revolution opened the way for a mass literature, and that the very machines which fashioned that age split romanticism into two factions, one of which continued the poetic revolution that the first generation had begun. To the other it presented new possibilities for artistic expression. It helped focus attention on prose, thereby aiding the shift from the romance to the novel and further contributed to the novelist a modern set of characters and themes; to both prose and poetry it gave new and striking images. In short, it was a major factor in the development of French romanticism.

Romanticism and Popular Culture

G. S. R. KITSON CLARK

G. S. R. Kitson Clark is a Fellow of Trinity College, Cambridge, and University Reader in Constitutional History. He is author of two books on Sir Robert Peel and recently of the *Making of Victorian England*, a call for revision of traditional views which has produced much favorable critical comment. The following essay also takes issue with traditional historiography, here emphasizing the importance of popular conceptions in the development of an understanding of Romanticism, as opposed to concentration solely upon the work of leading intellectuals.

THE truth of the matter is of course that in history there are no clear beginnings and endings. Origins are often unexpectedly early, survivals almost always stubborn and long dated, and anything that suggests that history can be cut into exclusive watertight compartments must be a falsification. Yet periods are a necessary convenience, and there is one fact which must remain true of any period however arbitrarily chosen; the men who lived through it did, at the least, all live at the same time, and they all lived in a mental atmosphere which is not that of the world of today.

Certainly the atmosphere, or perhaps it would be more correct to say the atmospheres, of any period are difficult to isolate and still harder to describe. Too often the only evidence available is that of impression, also they seem to change subtly and continuously, to differ for different sections of society but to modify one into another by indefinable degrees. Yet it is very bad history to ignore them. It is bad history to assemble the relevant facts, depict them with an unmitigated sharpness of outline and uncompromising minuteness of detail and then to suggest that contemporaries would base their actions on the way those facts appear to us. They could not have done so. They could not possibly have seen things like that. There would be unexpected blind spots and differences of perspective, and there would be a variety of tones and values contributed by the observer himself. In order to understand why dead men acted you must look with dead men's eyes and that means thinking with dead men's brains.

This, as every historian knows, is no easy task. It may be reasonably possible where a man's letters survive and there are fairly full memorials of what he did or was like as an individual; but for the bulk of humanity there are at best few records of individual actions, such letters as there were have long since gone into the dustbin and the last memories perished with the grandchildren. The desire to fill this blank leads to two temptations; one to fill the back of the stage with types, crudely painted lath and canvas figures which run easily in grooves, the other to believe rather trustfully that where no individual motive is known it is relatively easy to supply a simple economic one. . . .

There may, however, be another sup-

From "The Romantic Element — 1830–1850" by G. S. R. Kitson Clark in *Studies in Social History*, edited by J. H. Plumb, pp. 212–220; 223–232; 234–237. By permission of Longmans, Green & Company, Ltd.

plementary method of approach. It may be possible to recover something of the atmosphere in which men lived, and for this purpose there may exist evidence which reveals something even about those who have left no trace. For instance if what men wrote has perished, what they read, or men like them read, may not have perished with them. If what they said is lost, the speeches to which they listened with applause may still be on record. The pictures they saw and liked, their newspapers, their music, their architecture, their furniture, even their crockery, all these things may have their story to tell about the people themselves if we can only understand the language. These things formed the background against which they lived and expressed their preferences. To grasp this kind of evidence the political and social historian must make greater use of the assistance of the historians of art and literature than he has been wont to do. He must, however, use them with this proviso. The historians of art and literature have a natural preference for good art and valuable literature and those who produced them, the general historian cannot allow himself any such prejudice, he must jettison his own taste and remember that the most important evidence may by its very nature be supplied by what he personally most deplores.

Now the word which is most often used about the art and literature of the period between 1830 and 1850 is the word "romantic." It is what may be called "romantic" as an element in the thought and feeling of that time that I wish to investigate, not because it is the only element present — clearly it is not — but partly because it may well be the element which separates the minds of that period most markedly from our own. To do this it is necessary to come to terms with the word itself, and it is not a satisfactory word, since it sprawls uncomfortably over the late eighteenth and early nineteenth century, applied pretty generously to a good many ob-

viously different things. . . . However, the word does mean something, there are important common factors and basic connections to be discovered in most of the things which are called romantic, and possibly the best thing to do for present purposes is to suggest one or two common characteristics which may not unfairly be ascribed to romanticism in its later or nineteenth-century phase.

Perhaps the primary characteristic is the importance romanticism accords to emotion and imagination. The motions of the heart are apt to the considered to be of greater validity and interest than what may be called the motions of the head, that is than cold calculation, or that intellectual exercise which the eighteenth century had called "reason," or even those restricting influences which any age might call common sense. Emotion and imagination have the right of way. Art must be freed from convention, or from the classical tradition of balance and restraint, so that they may find free expression; conduct must be guided by emotion rather than by strict rule. As the importance of emotion is enhanced so necessarily is the importance of the human being who entertains the emotion. If feeling is to be the test, then the history of the man who feels is peculiarly interesting and significant, and so is the moment at which he experiences the emotion at its strongest. There is, therefore, an emphasis on the moment of intense feeling rather than on the long duller days and months that may follow, on action, on decisive choice, even on gesture rather than on results, on the profoundly experienced part rather than on the reasoned and organized whole. But it must be remembered that to the romantic the true nature of the whole is more likely to be revealed by experience and vision rather than by the dry comprehensive processes of analysis and calculation.

All this may be the grounds of a perfectly defensible philosophy, in fact does probably convey something important about the way reality should be approached or a scale of values discovered. Inevitably, however, it has its weaker side. If classicism and rationalism deteriorate into dullness, superficiality and intolerable complacency, romanticism turns into silliness. The pleasures of emotion for the sake of emotion become dangerously attractive, and they are catered for by the extravagances of imagination. In literature forced situations are produced in which probability, ethics and all delineation of character have been sacrificed for the sake of emotion. Strange creatures are called into being, the exile from humanity, the mysterious wanderer with obscure but violent feelings, the improbable hero or the maniac lover, simply to be the vehicles of interesting if uncontrollable emotion. The romantic tourist, spiritual or physical, will frequent places or periods where habits are likely to be strange, motives passionate and unusual or the scenery suitable, places such as the Apennines or Switzerland or the Middle East, or periods such as what men chose to believe had been the middle ages.

As a matter of fact the pot had boiled over earlier. The most excited period of romanticism was possibly before 1830. By 1830 Shelley was dead, Blake was dead, Byron was dead, and the heyday of the Minerva Press, which had produced so many novels of horror, was over. But the models remained and were copied; moreover this choice of scene and character touches on another, and abiding, characteristic of romanticism, or of one form of romanticism, its love of what lay outside the experience of the ordinary man. This may indeed explain the novels of high life of the "silver fork school" of the '20's and '30's, but the most obvious reservoir for the exotic was the past, or what could be presented as the past. Of course in the Gothic novels and the novels of horror the fiction that any imaginable historic conditions had been reproduced was extremely thin, this was fairyland or goblin land and pretty silly at that. But the romantic impetus had driven men beyond the gates of

the castle of Otranto into something more real, and more important. The loosening of imagination, the interest in what was different because it was different had sometimes led men to an emotional appreciation of the values and conditions of a past period which was profounder and more realistic than the old projection of fixed attitudes and common motives into any period that might be named. . . . The ballad supplied for romantic ears what seemed to be, what sometimes was, the voice of the past speaking in thrilling terms of exciting things. They powerfully assisted the romantic conception of history; and, since ballads were of the folk and therefore essentially national, they as powerfully assisted what was perhaps the most important product of romantic history, the vision of nationalism, the deepened imaginative conception of the significant past and peculiar identity of a particular nation.

That conception was pregnant with future consequences. However, the past so realized was not the past of the scientific historian. It was the past with too much poetry put in, too much prose left out; that was after all what men wanted, for they had no desire to exchange the commonplace of their own day for the commonplace of another. This, however, emphasizes the third characteristic of romanticism. It is in general a literature of dissatisfaction, of escape or revolt and the last two terms can easily merge into each other. At its lowest this leads to a mere craving for the sensational and the macabre. At its highest it is the revolt of men profoundly dissatisfied with a shallow intellectualism which disdained emotion, or the intolerable complacency of a society which was at the same time artificial, self-satisfied and unjust. Of course revolt inspired by the attraction of the past might take the form of reaction, the contrast of a supposedly glorious yesterday with an undeniably sordid today. . . . If romanticism had taught men to contrast, to imagine or to feel, then the feelings which the world of the nineteenth century was most likely to excite were disgust, pity and anger.

The vision was stabilized and solidified by the fact that in the nineteenth century a favourite instrument of literature was the novel. The novels of Victor Hugo, George Sand, even Eugène Sue and certainly Charles Dickens taught men to see and feel what the world was like and to protest against it; as the stories of William Carleton and the brothers Banim might have taught Englishmen something of what they sadly needed to know about Ireland. In fact in the forties in England a deeply valuable service was performed for Englishmen by the social novelists, such as Disraeli, Charles Kingsley, Mrs. Gaskell and the humbler "Charlotte Elizabeth," who taught men much that they needed to know about industrialism. . . .

The period 1830 to 1850 runs roughly from the first Reform Bill to the eve of the Great Exhibition. It was a period of great expectations and of as great and as reasonable fears. Until the repeal of the Corn Laws in 1846, or possibly till the Chartist fiasco in 1848, the weather was stormy. Party strife was very bitter, elections corrupt and tumultuous, and both in England and Ireland there was intermittent but noisy popular agitation. This was not unnatural in a country hard pressed by the problems created by an enormously increased population, by new, and often harsh, methods in industry, by hope and suffering and by new ideas. As a result there was a feeling of strain. The situation engaged the anxious attention of some because they were painfully and personally involved, of others as ring-side spectators a little too near a rather indeterminate ring.

But it was not only the urgency of politics or of the economic situation that served to fill and excite men's minds in the thirties and forties. A main point in the case is that there was probably a larger reading public than ever before. The improvements in the printing press, particu-

larly the introduction by Koenig between 1810 and 1814 of the impression cylinder and flat-bed driven by steam had enormously increased the amount of printed matter which could be produced, and the eagerness with which such inventions were taken up suggests a great hunger for things to read which probably grew by what it fed upon. The newspapers had increased in number and importance, and would certainly have increased still further if it had not been for the stamp duties. But it was not only newspapers that were being printed. The development of circulating libraries in the eighteenth century had created a taste for novels. The great popularity of Scott and Byron and in due course of Dickens showed that there was a large public to be gained. . . . There were novels, there were books of travel, many works on religion, and by the 1830's a great many periodical reviews to cater for different sections of opinion. . . .

Who all these readers were it would be difficult to say, or, with any exactness, what their numbers were, since the habit of borrowing from libraries probably vitiates circulation figures. The problem of literacy is a difficult one, and possibly the working class reader was a class apart. One thing, however, is likely, the reading public was probably more sharply divided up into sections than it is now. . . . Sentiments not unlike those heard from the stage and the platform were repeated with flashing eye and curling lip by the heroes of novels. "Fiction," said Bulwer, ". . . is the oratory of literature." He was talking of the sensationalism of the lesser novelists. The great imaginative literature of the day, Carlyle, Dickens and the Brontës is of course, with lapses, in general of an infinitely higher intellectual calibre, yet the same upthrust of emotion is there and the same appeal to the passions. . . .

An equally significant factor is the great company of poets. Tennyson was only beginning to make his mark and there were complaints that no great poet had arisen to interpret the age, but if so it was not for want of trying, for the number of people writing poetry is beyond count. . . .

No doubt there were a variety of reasons for this outpouring. It was very easy to publish. Publishers, particularly local publishers, seem to have been ready to produce single volumes by unknown poets at only a trifling cost to the author, and there were a great many magazines which printed poetry. There was also by now a large number of models. There were Byron and Scott and Burns and Wordsworth to copy, and the whole apparatus of romanticism to use, chieftains, bards, lovers, wanderers, shipwrecks, spirits and the Swiss. . . .

The most important cause, however, remains behind. A great many people wrote because a great many people wanted to write, and what is more surprising a great many people wanted to read what they, or some of them, had written. They wanted the cloudy enthusiastic metaphysics, the sensational religiosity, the medievalism and the appeals to the heart. Some things they wanted because they fitted in with the fashion of the time, and others because they were what a large part of the public has always wanted and still asks for. One reason for the force of the romantic movement was its ability to find forms to gratify instincts which have always existed, and to destroy inhibitions which prevented their free play. This tendency may also have been assisted by the size and nature of the reading public which new facilities in publishing and printing called into being. In our own day the taste for the lachrymose and the taste for excitement even when conveyed by unbelievable characters in impossible situations has been well catered for by the cinema and is being taken over by television. It was then gratified by the sensational novel and the poet who specialized in the luxury of tears and the thought of death. . . .

. . . The tide of sentiment was at the flood, it had poured not only into the weakest literature but into the best, even into the work of some of the major critics. Thackeray spent a good deal of time laughing at the weaknesses of the literature of the day. . . . Yet in his own writings, Thackeray was himself a sentimentalist, nor was he impregnable to sentiment in other people's. His praise of the description of the death of Paul Dombey still excites wonder and terror, when it is remembered what that passage is like; it should be compared with the tears shed by Jeffrey, the scourge of poets, over the death of little Nell. Of course Dickens himself wanted, sometimes outrageously, to make people cry, he wanted to teach the superiority of those who feel over the coldhearted like Scrooge, Mr. Dombey or Mr. Gradgrind who could only calculate. It is an important lesson, one that an age that had inherited a great deal of gross callousness and brutality needed rather badly to learn, but it was not at that time an unpopular one, for it was much the same as was taught by many writers in the Christmas annuals. . . .

. . . What significant results derive from this exuberance? Much of this literature — the minor poetry, the sensational novelists, much even of Dickens himself — is of the dregs of romanticism, the sentiment shallow and mawkish, the "big words" and heavy emphasis bombastic and unconvincing. Probably these efforts were popular, the playthings of the day for those who liked that sort of thing, but they seem to be as little likely to excite deep or lasting emotion as they were high art. If so is their popularity of any importance? What is there here which a serious historian should take into account as one of the important operative factors of the period?

The question is not easy. It raises the difficult question whether what is admittedly trivial, produced to fill an idle moment with facile emotion or excitement, does not yet reveal something of the mind that likes to be amused in that way. But the phrase "admittedly trivial" begs a still harder question. It is difficult to know what it is permissible to dismiss as trivial and superficial; the touchstone of what we hold to be good taste may be in such matters the worst of guides. What began as a plaything may very easily come to symbolize something much more important. The passion for medievalism was probably in the eighteenth century mainly a whim, and in the 1830's was producing such things as the novels of G. P. R. James, which are but readable fustian, and many "a tale of olden time," which is undoubted rubbish. It was also filling the country with a great deal of very mediocre architecture and many objects of quite disastrous design. Yet to Pugin it was the symbol of important values, it probably profoundly affected the religious history of the country. It was the source of political idealism to men like the enthusiasts of "Young England," and encouraged an attitude to the past which instructed the ideas of others who have made a much deeper mark than they upon the history of Europe.

Moreover, what seems to be unquestionably trivial and superficial to us is of precisely the same nature as what touched on matters of unquestionable importance. The sentimentalism which was gratified by the fate of little Nell or by the various songs and poems about orphans is not easily distinguishable from the sentiment that instructed men and women what to think about the negro slave, the factory child or the boy chimney sweep. It was indeed stimulated by much the same techniques. As has been suggested the bombast in the novels and on the stage bears a close family resemblance to the overvehemence of public speakers in the various agitations, moral or political, of the twenty years after the Reform Bill. . . .

. . . The tone of much contemporary journalism, the methods and vehemence of much contemporary controversy, the style of much contemporary religion — all these things combine to suggest that in his dealings with this period a historian must take into account an emotionalism which was more general and more easily excited than anything he knows today. If that is so he must learn to recognize the words, the ideas, the associations, the literary forms, which were then likely to stimulate strong emotions and would not do so today.

He must at the same time realize that the same stimulants did not have the same effect on all sections of the community. Certain types of systematic thought would reject them, the necessary realism of many occupations would deaden them, aristocratic traditions make them seem nauseating or absurd. . . . The Duke of Wellington seems to have been immune, and so too were probably not a few of the nobility and gentry to be found on the benches of either house of parliament, so too to an exemplary extent were the Benthamites, so too were many manufacturers or farmers in matters that strictly concerned their business.

These men were important since in their hands lay many of the keys of power. Yet there were many not affected by these counterbalances, or to whom the literary fashions of the day seemed to give profound utterance to what was most important in life. For instance in the lower ranges of literature and art religious motifs were prominent. . . .

There is, however, a matter of deeper significance here. In the eighteenth century there had been the great Evangelical revival, and though by 1830 the tide was ebbing, it had not ebbed very far. Now Evangelical Christianity seems to satisfy all the categories of romanticism, except the love of fancy dress. It, too, was an appeal to vital emotion. . . . Each in his own way, men like Rousseau and men like John Wesley had taught men to look into their own hearts to find truths and values that an overcivilized, over-intellectualized, society had never known or had forgotten. To look within is always exciting, and the results may be explosive.

The Evangelical revival had spread into every class and corner of England, from the lowest to the highest. . . .

Its moral force remained effective and widely diffused, so also was its power of well-savoured moral denunciation. It provided for much of the nation an ethical code, strongly enforced by emotion, for general reference; more than this of all forms of romanticism it was the best organized. The first really effective nation-wide organization to secure one particular political object was the agitation against slavery and the slave trade organized by the Clapham Saints. They canvassed the whole country, and gave to many what was possibly their first taste in romanticism, a stirring emotional experience and an interest in unhappy far-off things. It was the forerunner of many moral agitations which supplied a spice to the lives of many who thought the drama was sinful. But it was not only religious agitations that it inspired; when Cobden was meditating his attack on the Corn Laws he came explicitly to the conclusion that success would be his if he turned it into a great moral movement like the agitation against slavery. . . .

But the emotional stimuli available for politics were by no means all of them religious. Romantic literature was full of the struggles of the heroes of liberty, such as Rienzi or William Tell; it abounded in such poetry as Byron addressed to the Greeks, or Burns to the Scots who had bled with Wallace, and, as has been said before, it gave force and reality to a resurgent nation's vision of itself. Scotland was rediscovered, almost reinvented round the eccentric nucleus of the Highlander; but possibly the classical example of the application of literary romanticism to emergent nationalism was in Ireland, in the forties. . . .

. . . The results were likely to be violent. The idea of force has a strong literary and dramatic attraction and, as in America so in Ireland, literary romanticism was bellicose. . . .

In England with Chartism the literary background is different, for romantic nationalism would not have been relevant, but the same issue emerged there between those Chartists who advocated moral and those who advocated physical force; and the speeches of the physical force men — Stephens, Feargus O'Connor, McDouall and Harney — provide interesting examples of romantic oratory. They also draw attention to an interesting problem which is also present in Ireland, the relation of what is mere literary form to what is a not unreasonable appreciation of the real situation. On the one hand many orators are using language in which appeals to dread alternatives, just vengeance, or liberty or death, are almost a literary convention, but on the other hand the misery of sections of the working class in England and the peasantry in Ireland was so great and the obduracy with which redress seemed to be refused was so impregnable that without that stimulus men might understandably come to believe that violence was the only resort. . . .

Yet if both in England and Ireland the realities of the situation justified the romantic approach, there were some realities that the romantic approach did not normally reveal. It did not encourage a cool appraisal of chances, or the careful preparations which are necessary for the use of force, or even a very clear appreciation of what words about force really implied. As with most forms of emotionalism the eloquent moment overshadowed the problem of what might follow. The Chartists flirted with violence, they talked about it, they never adequately prepared for it, and many of those who threatened it never consistently or realistically intended it; when challenged by the law both Feargus O'Connor and Joseph Stephens explained that they had not really meant what they appeared to have said, which was probably true. . . .

If this diagnosis is correct there was then in these twenty years an atmosphere more heavily charged with emotion than anything we know. That emotion was potent, it had revived religion and was forming morals, it could enliven politics, it could revivify nationalism, it taught men to feel and to understand the lot of the less fortunate and to stand up for their own wrongs, if not to understand what was meant by armed revolt. It is also seeped into poor drama and not very good painting, into death-bed literature, or silly novels, or into religion at the level of the oleograph and of those hymns which present no real personal experience, no statement of dogma, but are mere collections of well-tried stimuli for the easier feelings. Whence it came might be a difficult question. Some part of the answer has been suggested; it came partly from the exciting, often distressing, situation of the moment, partly from the unchanging appetites of the human mind gratified and excited by the prevaling passion for oratory, and by the fact that the ingenuity of inventors, the enterprise of publishers, the fertility of authors had given so many of them so much that was so suitable for them to read.

But behind all this, through all this, sweeps that mysterious tidal wave which passed through Europe, which men have called romanticism. Only, to be properly understood, romanticism must be considered not only as something which affected some of the leading minds of the day, it must be considered as a popular movement, even a vulgar movement; with the expressions of exalted politics and important thought must be read much that was ephemeral and seems to us absurd. But the case is that, when all these things are considered, they present an element in the public mind which cannot be disregarded by those who desire to understand how men thought or why they acted.

Response to Contemporary Crisis

EUGENE N. ANDERSON

Eugene N. Anderson is a specialist in German history who has taught at the University of Chicago, at American University, at the University of Nebraska and at the University of California, Los Angeles. In the following essay, Anderson views German Romanticism as a response to the crises, intellectual, political, and social, which Germany faced in the Revolutionary era.

THE Romantic movement in Germany accompanied and expressed one reaction to the social transformation from the culture of caste and absolutism to that of class and constitutional rule. The Romanticists sought to formulate the ideals of a society in the making. While dependent for lack of practical experience upon aesthetics or ethics for their basic standards, they strove to compass the whole of life.

The influence of the French Revolution greatly accelerated the social changes in Germany and stimulated the young German Romanticists to an outburst of creativeness in all phases of life. The decade or so beginning in the last half of the 1790s saw the culmination of movements already under way in both the socio-political and the aesthetic-intellectual spheres. The participants in each spurred on those in the other, and in this short time of crisis, cultural forms and directions which have conditioned German life down to the present were fixed. In reflecting the characteristics of the crisis, Romanticism manifested, sometimes in exaggerated ways, those of the cultural change which the crisis brought to a head.

During these few years the young German Romanticists felt the danger to German culture from the French Revolution and Napoleon to be less political than intellectual and spiritual, and they endeavored to oppose it by ideas. While considering all aspects of life, including the political, they were especially concerned with the emancipation of individualities and the discovery of the manifold richness of the world. This period witnessed the fullest expression of German Romanticism as a total way of life. In the succeeding years the danger became acutely political, and the German Romanticists were compelled to subordinate their preoccupation with the widening of art and the enrichment of individual experience to social and political ideas and actions, particularly as formulated in nationalism and conservatism. These three cultural ideals, Romanticism, nationalism and conservatism, shared qualities evoked by the common situation of crisis; but by establishing exclusive, impersonal standards of value the latter two destroyed the unique features of their predecessor.

German Romanticism has usually been studied with a view to discovering its unique, differentiating features. While recognizing the value of these investigations, this essay will seek to exhibit in Romanticism certain common characteristics imposed upon the responses of individuals by the condition of cultural transformation and crisis. It will avoid definition in favor

From "German Romanticism as an Ideology of Cultural Crisis," by Eugene N. Anderson, in The Journal of the History of Ideas (June, 1941), pp. 301–317. By permission of the author and The Journal of the History of Ideas.

of cultural analysis. It will show how Romanticism used elements which, individually, were not peculiar to it alone, but which, brought into relationship by the situation, constituted the essential patterns of Romantic thought and action.

The young German Romanticists in the period under discussion, though differing on many points of detail, were all acutely aware of the fact that they lived in a time of swift transition from one culture to another. Their philosophizing about history and their describing of utopias manifested a deep concern with the problems of this cultural crisis; they wished to know where they stood in the course of history and where that course was taking them. The French Revolution, they thought, marked the dividing line between two ages, either as the past phase of the old age or as the first of the new, and they wished that German Romanticism should provide the essential forms for the future. The writers regarded themselves as media of expression of this culture, the coming of which they tended to regard as inevitable.

The fact of living in a time of cultural crisis conditioned the thinking and acting of the young German Romanticists as no other experience did. It forced them to deal not merely with a single aspect of life but with the totality of man, society, and the universe. The crisis involved all values; it affected not merely the parts of man's existence but the whole. While compelling each person to seek his own salvation as best he could, it also forced him to look for support from the group. In the decade or so beginning with the late 1790s Romanticism offered a way of deliverance for persons caught in a crisis.

As is to be expected, the fundamental ideology of German Romanticism has to do with the nature of the particular, of the whole, and of the relations between them. The Romanticists applied this ideology to every element in the world, whether man or divinity, family or nation, individual or state, peace or war, concept or book, speaker or audience, an act or an institu-

tion. The particular, they thought, should be an individual expression of the whole. . . .

If both the particular and the whole should be individualistic, each in its own way, the Romanticists had to find a means for bringing them into intimate relation. The difficulty which they confronted in doing so is attested to by the diverse formulations of their answer. In every case, however, the solution was fundamentally the same. . . . The Romantic solution to the problem of relationship between the particular and the whole may be summed up in the old formula, so paradoxical to rationalists: one serves the group best by realizing one's self most completely; one is most free when one is most willing to sacrifice one's self for the group. It is a formula with a dialectic as the core.

A society functioning at a fairly even pace would deny the practicality of such views; but to a people in a time of swift cultural change anything was possible. The Romanticists witnessed the destruction of forms and ways that had seemed eternal, the sudden upsurge of novelties of which they had only dreamed. With institutions collapsing, unknown men becoming rulers, boundaries made flexible, serfs obtaining freedom and property, with, in short, a condition of seemingly complete flux, the potentialities of the single individual expanded enormously. God no longer kindly came down to man, the Romanticists thought, but man could and should climb toward Heaven; transcending the restrictions of mere rationality man could and should become a total personality, a complete unity of body, mind and soul, the image of the universe. The Romanticists were exaggerating and universalizing the emancipating and exciting characteristics of the first phase of a cultural crisis.

By undermining standards while at the same time stimulating emotional and thought processes, the crisis led the Romanticists to explore the metaphysical and religious bases of ideas and practices.

The early maturity of individuals which the situation of swift cultural change entailed turned their attention upon the profoundest questions of life and death, of the state and nation, of personality and of God. Taking seriously Kant's epistemological dualism, many of them refused to be deprived of the *Ding-an-sich* and asserted the reality of both the sensuous and the supernatural world. The relationship between the particular and the total grew so rich and complex that it could only be expressed by a symbol. The mystery of the God-man became laicised and universalized; mystery entered into the simplest thing; even the state, the Romanticists thought, should reach its highest character by becoming poetic. Romanticism reflected the astonishment evoked by the extraordinary events of these years of crisis. Could human beings alone, even though exalted as they should be, have brought about the French Revolution, transformed European culture, opened up a new era? The most incredible act seemed the most credible. . . .

The search for realities focussed the Romanticists' attention upon the process of living. The speed with which things were changing around them, the importance of organic force in conditioning these changes, the zest and excitement of so much action, heightened their appreciation of the sheer fact of being alive. Everything seemed in movement, man, nature, God, and the historic results of their work. Referring repeatedly to the educative influence of the crisis, Adam Müller shaped his theory to the fact of living movement. He condemned all previous analyses of the state and of political economy for having dealt with these institutions in a condition of peace. He declared that in peaceful times egocentricity and materialism dominate the individual, the state falls apart, and the theorist describes a situation of decay. The present crisis had shown the circumstances, he said, in which the state becomes completely itself. It must be in the natural condition of simultaneous peace and war, when each element in the state fulfills its total potentialities and merges with all the others in a common purpose and a common life. Since Müller was fashioning his ideas in the crisis situation, he screwed up his courage by claiming universal validity for them. European revolutions and wars demanded such furious living, such strenuous defense of the right to live, that the Romanticists rushed to the extreme position of regarding these conditions as normal, or of believing that, if they were not normal, they should be. The conception of the state as of the personality expressed the Romanticists' proposals for coping with the plight of the times. It reflected an excessive concern with the organic and the living, with movement and action, with the total steeling of one's self for the rigors of this swift-changing age.

The cultural crisis produced sinister effects as well, and these had to be overcome. The individual became uprooted, isolated, anxious. The uncertainty excited his nerves and strained his emotions. He confronted a world of turmoil and danger, the harsh impact of unexpected forces. He became remarkably sensitive to problems of relationship with elements — human or otherwise — which affected him, and he craved unity with those capable of aiding him. The Romanticists sought to assure themselves of intimacy with other individuals and with things in many ways. They made a cult of friendship; they lived together in intimate groups; they frequently collaborated with such harmony that they called the resulting work a child of their marriage. Literary forms using the spoken word were favored because of their personal quality. The Romanticists personalized all things, and put them in relationship with each other.

The longing for unity with others drove the Romanticists to glorify the family and the corporative social orders, gilds, estates, the church, hansas, republics, the state. . . . The monarch, the state and the nation occupied the most exalted places, for they related the other forms with humanity and with God. . . . The Romanticists recognized that the past could not be restored, and expressed ideals especially about the state which would preserve German culture in the present crisis and inaugurate the happy age to come. . . .

When the German Romanticists wrote about economic affairs, they started with the same objective in mind that they had in discussing all social forms. They wished to bind individuals together into a working unit. It was Adam Müller who most fully applied these conceptions in the economic sphere, asserting that even landed property had mobility; and he weighed the significance of things, as he did that of persons, according to the influence which these things or persons exercised in society. . . .

The German Romanticists shared with the nationalists a common distrust of guidance of human action by reason. No rational institution, no man-made association would reassure them, for they had seen these fail in the French Revolution. The insecurity which results from a condition of cultural transition forced the Romanticists to exalt those forms in which relationships are based on irrational ties, marriage, the family, organism (if not taken too literally), and to use them as models for less closely knit institutions like the state. They attributed to man the instincts and drives by means of which complete unity with others would be achieved. Görres and Eichendorff spoke of the "instinct of freedom," of "loyalty," of "obedience," of "loving devotion." In every case the Romantic assumptions about the nature of man are fundamentally the same, and in every case the power of love suffuses these instinct-driven individuals and binds them irrevocably together. The uncertainty and insecurity of the period were counter-balanced by the super-charged emotionality of romantic love; the easy relations of the rococo period tightened into these close bonds. Excessive danger to the individual in a society in travail called

forth the unusual demand for support, the reassurance of love from others. The Romanticists' thoughts and feelings focussed upon love; their most profound experience was that of love. . . . Irrational and transcendental powers, the heart and the spirit, the poetic and the philosophic, enabled each individual, isolated, uncertain, anxious, to realize oneness with the group.

The speed of cultural change, the occurrence of so many unexpected events, also awakened in the Romanticists a profound sense of the significance of time. Living, movement, relation, time, these four elements constituted different aspects of the romantic Weltanschauung. The Romanticists had to live intensely while they could; they must compress into each occasion the totality of existence. A unit of time had a full life of its own. The sensitivity to the present was accentuated by the speed of its passing. But the rate of change also aroused within the Romanticists the longing for something which persisted. Duration seemed to them a basic standard of value. Institutions, in which time condensed, preserved the wisdom of human experience, and tradition and custom revealed transcendental powers. The spirit of the folk spoke through them and kept men from erring too far from the laws of God and nature. The analogy of the live being portrayed the relation between present, past and future. The sense of past time led to the study of history and the wish to preserve one's heritage; it disclosed fixed values and lent assurance as to the course of mankind. The sense of future time made one aware of one's responsibility for that which was to come and to desire reform for its sake. The living thing endures for its allotted time, leaves its imprint, and passes away. It harmonizes the qualities of movement and duration; the inorganic does not. The Romanticists, eager to be themselves in an age of seeming chaos, everywhere applied the conception of a living individuality.

When movement is so pervasive it demands explanation. The Romanticists' acute awareness of the changes going on was manifested in their abiding concern with this problem. The explained change by means of the dialectic and the theory of opposites, which in spite of variations in emphasis and detail essentially conformed to a pattern. "Unity can never be represented except in diversity," wrote Adam Müller, "or diversity except in unity." The Romanticists were describing to their own satisfaction that which seemed to occur around them. In the crisis the one extreme generated a contrary extreme; a new form arose, only to initiate the process all over again. The theory afforded great comfort to a society in the course of disintegration. The inevitable functioning of the dialectic even relieved the individual of responsibility for social action. The natural law of opposites would restore the righteous and destroy the wicked. It assured the Romanticists of the victory of their revolution against the French Revolution; the living ideal would conquer the dead one, humanity would enter an age in which the ideas fundamental for cultural creativeness would be restored to power and would guide mankind along the path of eternal progress. The worse conditions became, the more optimistic Adam Müller felt, for he recognized the infallible sign of speedy revival.

The situation in Germany seemed especially favorable to the flowering of Romanticism. Although classicism had taken vigorous hold of German intellectual life, especially in the eighteenth century, as contrasted with France and Italy the influence had endured for a relatively short time. The classical culture provided for the Romance countries the fundamental elements which the Gothic tradition did for Germany. The German Romanticists attached themselves to this tradition, and feared that the flourishing intellectual and spiritual life in Germany might be harmed or destroyed by French domination. The German people could scarcely have initiated a revolution in the name of rationalism, for they lacked any means of unified

public action. An Estates General could not have convened in Germany, or even in that accumulation of territories, Prussia. The German revolution took the form of a countermovement against the revolution in France. From the beginning German Romanticism sought to defend German culture against the French Enlightenment; a few years of experience with the French Revolution aroused the young Romanticists actively and ardently to oppose their ideals to it. Conservatism was implicit in German Romanticism, not in the sense of any subsequent political party, but as a potential attitude. One can defend or conserve any type of social system. The Germans had to maintain against rationalism and the French a culture which in its institutional structure was that of the *ancien régime*. German Romanticism accepted it, wished to reform it somewhat, idealized it, and defended the idealization as the supreme culture of the world. This was the German counterrevolution.

The individuals who formulated the Romantic ideals constituted a relatively small number of intellectuals. That they originated in various social groups, and in both Protestant and Catholic circles, attests to the emancipating and stimulating effect of a situation of crisis. These persons of diverse backgrounds could most readily come together around ideals which romanticized the institutional *status quo*. Their criticism of rationalism as incomplete was in conformity with the irrationality of the crisis, and the Romantic desire to recognize realities and the need for the union of all in defending German culture against the French Enlightenment and the Revolution strengthened this attitude. The acute menace to the German way of life led to the exaltation of this way to the point of divinity. The Romanticists even consecrated to defensive purposes the belief in cosmopolitanism, the one respect in which the German had escaped from the essential control of the German cultural structure. They endowed their culture with universal validity and asserted that it enjoyed the devotion of nature and God, that if it were destroyed humanity would be vitally wounded.

The condition of swift cultural transition favored the ideals and activities of youth and early manhood. The opportunities for achieving great things seemed limitless; if the individual would seize them, his throbbing heart (one had no time for the drudgery of rationalistic study), his enthusiasm joined with some talent promised success. Youth thought it could create or seek new, subjective values in harmony with its emotions. Faustian passion drove it to compass all life, past, present, and future, and it felt anarchy to be the generative ground of its perfection. Exaggerations and superlatives belong to youth and crisis, and they belong to Romanticism.

The Romanticists were as active as circumstances allowed. To accuse them of aesthetic idleness, or to condemn them for not having been Bismarcks or hard capitalists seems grossly unfair. In the areas open to them they lived strenuously, turning out numerous books, establishing and editing magazines, trying many forms of expression, absorbing many varieties of knowledge. The devotion to the blue flower did not reduce their energy. Scarcely any age in history has been more productive in writing and music, or more fertile in ideas. The Romanticists even wished eagerly to be politically important, and when the War of Liberation broke out, they used their powers to the full in fighting and in propaganda. It took courage to denounce Napoleon and to exalt the Germans, to be partisan in internal conflicts over reforms. The Romanticists showed far more bravery than many of their carping contemporaries. None the less, it is true that in their trust in spiritual values, the Romanticists easily inclined to substitute ideals for material and political realities. Ideals narcotized these young enthusiasts against the unpleasant features of the time and secured them a retreat in the romantic world of their own making. The Romanticists compensated for the weakness of

earthly forces by belief in the enormous strength of transcendental power. Wishing ideal and practice to harmonize, they could consummate the union most easily in the realm of imagination. The crisis stimulated the traffic in ideas, which, like Romantic interest in magic, might provide short-cuts to security; but it did not favor systematization, and the stress upon guidance by feeling reduced planning to relative insignificance.

The romantic ideal of identity and immanence has a conservative tendency. The belief that each object personifies in its particular way the total universe affords a total basis for a total defense of the individuality. The highest criterion of value to the Romanticist consisted in an individuality's containing its own justification, its own purpose. This view precluded any attack against the particular in the name of an objective standard. Where nature and God reveal themselves in the individual the defense seems complete. The German Romanticists were interested, not in the question of what to conserve, but rather in that of how to conserve it. Differing from the nationalists in that they recognized the nation as but one among many individualities, they provided the ideological foundation for the defensive union of all German groups against the French. The low estimate of rationalism and the exaltation of custom, tradition, and feeling, the conception of society as an alliance of the generations, the belief in the abiding character of ideas as contrasted with the ephemeral nature of concepts, these and many other romantic views bolstered up the existing culture. The concern with relations led the Romanticists to praise the hierarchical order of the *Ständestaat* [Corporative State] and to regard everything and everyone as an intermediary. The acceptance of the fact of inequality harmonized with that of the ideals of service, duty, faithfulness, order, sacrifice — admirable traits for serf or subject or soldier. . . .

During a crisis the Romantic dialectic

assists the elements of change or reform but also those of conservatism. Where there is freedom, there must be counter-freedom; where equality, inequality; where a follower, a leader; where movement, stability. Multiplicity of forms is necessary for completeness; out of the inter-action of opposites God and nature create life. The *ancien régime,* with its variety of estates, privileges, ways and customs of many ages and many places, offered a fruitful soil for the creative functioning of the dialectic. Adam Müller expressed the Romantic will to stand above partisan-ship and find the true answer in the posi-tion of the higher third, the mate to Hegel's synthesis. By this means the Ro-manticists provided authoritarianism with a natural and divine foundation. The crisis-situation might accelerate the work-ing of the opposites and stimulate rapid cultural change; but the dialectic sanc-tioned strong resistance to change even during the crisis. Once the latter had passed, the dialectic ceased to express a social need, and if preserved as a theory it was made to function so slowly that a single cultural system could appear as a norm.

The Romantic conception of relationship postulates the presence of two original ele-ments, the particular and the whole. When this theory is applied to society, it may easily lead to a struggle for supremacy be-tween them. Appreciating the threat of the superior force of the whole over the partic-ular, Romantic writers enhanced the sig-nificance of the latter to the point of being a totality in itself. During a crisis the freedom of the creative particular is vital, and the Romanticists praised it with en-thusiasm. None the less, the whole pre-serves its potential power, and the Roman-ticists tended to ignore the fact that it might be dominated by an absolute mon-arch, a self-centered aristocracy, deter-mined to maintain as fully as possible the existing social structure. One half of the relationship might do its part in the crisis while the other obstructed the efforts to free the individualities for action. The polarity between individual freedom and initiative and group compulsion and au-thority was one which the Romanticists were never able to escape. They remained swinging between the two extremes. But society, which was organized around group institutions, found the issue easier to de-cide: it simply preserved most of the group institutions, by sheer force of inertia, and the individual had to conform. That was the case in Germany.

The Romantic theory functions only if aggressive leaders like Stein are present, leaders who feel with the Romanticists the effects of the crisis situation but who bring to this situation a rich, practical experi-ence. The Romanticists themselves could not have executed fundamental reforms. By reverencing tradition, they preserved the power of the backward-looking royalty and aristocracy. The threat of conserva-tism and restoration lay in constant attend-ance upon the active individuality. The Romantic ideal tended to intoxicate a group of intellectuals in a cultural crisis. It was admirably suited to the risky position of a bureaucrat-professor or a writer eager for state favor: it could be either radical or conservative, idealistic or realistic, accord-ing to need; it beautified and transcen-dentalized Prussian society; it could mean to everyone that which he wished it to mean without running much danger of modifying the *status quo.* It was as so-cially safe an ideal as could appear in a crisis.

On the whole the Romantic leaders did not claim to be messiahs. Their effort to know reality and their view of all persons and things not as isolated units but as intermediaries (Mittler) between others intimately related to them, indicate a cer-tain modesty. Those among them who in-clined to estimate their historic importance at an usually high rate were of burgher or peasant origin. Loose from their social bases, they strove toward position and fame. Since political activity was practi-cally closed to them, and since the economic opportunities open to a burgher were meagre and carried a social stigma, they chose the somewhat irresponsible and specious career of a writer. During the crisis, they rose with the rising power of ideas; but materially and psychologically they remained dependent upon the institutional *status quo*. As they grew older, they lost the youthful capacity for romantic enthusiasm. By the time Napoleon crushed Austria and Prussia, they were already transferring their interest from personal problems to social and political ones. They were discovering that some things were worth fighting for. While their work contributed to the Stein-Hardenberg reforms, it also furthered the Junker resistance against these reforms. The Romanticists began to repudiate their own ideals. They began to seek solace and security in revelation, to revere form and authoritarianism. Catholicism, which shared so many common characteristics with Romanticism, afforded a refuge for some. After 1815 the Restoration served a similar need. Transcendental dogma, either religious or secular, gave these footloose intellectuals the solid basis which caste and property provided for the aristocracy and the throne for royalty. Romanticism as a full way of life lasted as long as the cultural crisis favored the ferment of ideas and the accompanying enthusiastic optimism.

The ideology of Romanticism became as traditional for Germany as that of the French Revolution for France. Much of German history during the past century pertains to the search for unity and defense. Much of it portrays the struggle of the forces of the *ancien régime,* so powerful in Germany, against industrial capitalism. German conservatism, liberalism and socialism alike were affected by the persistence of this cultural conflict and in greater or less degree absorbed elements of Romanticism. In a nation which through centuries had acquired the habits of particularism, Romanticism offered the best ideological means for drawing together the diverse elements. Whenever a crisis threatened or occurred, Romantic theory reappeared.

SUGGESTIONS FOR ADDITIONAL READING

The student who has confronted the variety of interpretations of Romanticism suggested by the readings in this volume will desire first of all to examine the major works of the leading figures of the Romantic era. Selections of Romantic writing appear in innumerable anthologies. Useful collections which offer works translated from foreign languages include: Eugen Weber, *Paths to the Present, Aspects of European Thought from Romanticism to Existentialism* (New York, 1960), an excellent paperbound collection containing especially useful sources from France; Howard E. Hugo's *Viking Portable Romantic Reader* (New York, 1957) offers a skillfully edited exemplification of American, English, French, and German writings. Angel Flores has edited *An Anthology of German Poetry from Hölderlin to Rilke* (Garden City, New York, 1960); *Nineteenth Century German Tales* (Garden City, New York, 1959); *An Anthology of French Poetry from Nerual to Valery* (Garden City, New York, 1958) and *Nineteenth Century French Tales* (Garden City, New York, 1960). Recent collections of English Romantic writings easily available include: Raymond Wright, ed., *Prose of the Romantic Period 1780–1830* (London, 1956); Carl R. Woodring ed., *Prose of the Romantic Period* (Boston, 1961); and George R. Creeger and Joseph W. Reed, Jr., eds., *Selected Prose and Poetry of the Romantic Period* (New York, 1964) — which last offers an intriguing combination of poetry and criticism. Textbook anthologies of English Romantic poetry, in fact, the works of major English authors (Wordsworth, Coleridge, Shelley, Byron, Keats, Lamb, Hazlitt, DeQuincey, etc.) are available so readily and in so many editions (including recent paperback editions) that they require no listing.

Major writings of the leading continental literary Romanticists are also available in translation in a variety of editions. Among such works, the following are recommended: for Italian Romanticism, Manzoni's *The Betrothed* (New York, 1951) and Leopardi's Poems in *Translations from Leopardi* (Cambridge, 1951); for Germany, Goethe's *Faust* (e.g., Penguin, Modern Library, Rinehart, etc. editions), *The Poetry and Prose of Heinrich Heine,* ed., Frederick Ewen (New York, 1948); and Novalis, *Hymns to the Night and Other Selected Writings* (New York, 1960); for Russia, Lermontov's *A Hero for Our Time* (Garden City, New York, 1958); for France, Rousseau's *Confessions* in the Penguin Classics (London, 1960), Stendhal's *Scarlet and Black* in the same series (London, 1955); and Chateaubriand's *Atala and René* (New York, 1961).

Among the most important writings of the early nineteenth century for the student of Romanticism are those which defined or sought to define the new views of life and art. Particularly significant are Wordsworth's "Preface" to *Lyrical Ballads,* Mme. de Staël's *Germany* (New York, 1859), Heinrich Heine's counterstatement which appeared in his *Germany,* available in translation in *The Works of Heinrich Heine* (London, 1891–1905), Victor Hugo's "Preface" to *Cromwell,* which is translated in Harvard Classics (New York, 1909–10), Shelley's "Defence of Poetry," and Stendhal's *Racine and Shakespeare* (New York, 1962).

In the areas of politics and philosophy, for Britain Burke's writings probably should be examined first, supplemented by Coleridge *On the Constitution of the Church and State,* Disraeli's novels, especially *Sybil,* Newman's *Apologia Pro Vita Sua,* and the chief writings of Carlyle. For the continent, H. S. Reiss has edited a useful selection of translations in *The Political Thought of the German Romantics 1793–1815* (New York, 1955). Of course for this period the Germans were preeminent in formal philosophy and produced much of the most original romantic speculation in religion. Suggested works in translation are Fichte's *The Vocation of Man* and Herder's *God, Some Conversations*, both from Liberal Arts Press, 1940 and 1956; Schelling's *Of Human Freedom* (Chicago, 1936), and Schleiermacher's *On Religion: Speeches to Its Cultured Despisers* (available in recent paperback editions). Study of French thought in this period should begin with Rousseau. Other representative works available in translation are, e.g., DeMaistre *On God and Society*, ed. Elish Greifer (Chicago, 1959); Lamartine, *History of the French Revolution of 1848* (Boston, 1857); Lamennais, *Words of a Believer* (New York, 1834), and Fourier, in *Selections from the Works of Fourier* (London, 1901). Two figures whose works most strikingly represent romantic nationalism are Mazzini, available in translation in the Everyman's Library edition of *The Duties of Man and Other Essays* (London, 1955), and Mickiewicz, a selection from whose works can be found in *Selected Poetry and Prose*, centenary edition (New York, 1955).

Interesting secondary treatments of these areas include J. H. Talmon's *Political Messianism, The Romantic Phase* (New York, 1960); Reinhold Aris, *Political Thought in Germany 1789–1815* (London, 1936); Crane Brinton, *Political Ideas of the English Romantics* (Oxford, 1926); Basil Willey, *Nineteenth Century Studies* (London, 1949); Peter Viereck, *Metapolitics: From the Romantics to Hitler* (New York, 1941); D. O. Evans, *Social Romanticism in France, 1830–1848* (New York, 1952). For philosophy and science, see G. H. Mead, *Movements of Thought in the Nineteenth Century* (Chicago, 1936); and especially

for Britain, Alfred North Whitehead, *Science and the Modern World* (New York, 1948).

Romantic historiography has been brilliantly treated by Emery Neff in *The Poetry of History* (New York, 1961). See also R. G. Collingwood, *The Idea of History* (Oxford, 1946). The historical writings of such figures as Carlyle and Michelet will repay examination.

A volume such as the present one does not lend itself to intensive treatment of music and the plastic arts. Major writings of the period which will supplement the study of the painting and music it produced are such works as the *Autobiography and Memoirs of Benjamin Robert Haydon* (London, 1926); the *Journal of Eugene Delacroix* (Hubert Wellington, ed., Phaedon Press, London, 1951) and Charles Baudelaire's *The Mirror of Art* (Garden City, 1956) for painting; and for music, the *Letters, Journals and Conversations* of Beethoven, edited by Michael Hamburger (Garden City, New York, 1962) and the *Memoirs* of Berlioz (New York, 1935). There is of course a rich secondary literature in these areas. Of particular note is Jacques Barzun's biography, *Berlioz and the Romantic Century* (Boston, 1950). Histories and special studies of painting include: Geraldine Pelles, *Art, Artists & Society, Origins of a Modern Dilemma* (Englewood Cliffs, New Jersey, 1963), Walter Friedlander, *David to Delacroix* (Cambridge, 1952), K. Clark, *The Gothic Revival*, 2nd ed. (London, 1950), Marcel Brion, *Romantic Art* (New York, 1950). For music see Paul Henry Lang, *Music in Western Civilization* (New York, 1941), and A. Einstein, *Music in the Romantic Era* (New York, 1947).

General historical assessments and evaluations of Romanticism have been less numerous than narrower critical writings about the works of the period. Such critical writing anent English romanticism has been conveniently exemplified in *Romanticism: Points of View*, Robert Gleckner and Gerald Enscoe, eds., (Englewood Cliffs, N. J., 1962). A few further major critical treatments include, for England, Walter Jackson Bate, *From Classic to Romantic* (Boston, 1946) and Hoxie Neale Fairchild, *The Noble Savage, A Study in Romantic Naturalism* (New York, 1928); for Germany, L. A. Willoughby, *The Romantic Movement in Germany* (London, 1930), and R. Tymms, *German Romantic Literature* (London, 1955); and for France, André Maurois' biographies of such figures as Hugo and Chateaubriand are brilliant and sympathetic. A recent effort to comprehend the whole movement is Morse Peckham's *Beyond the Tragic Vision* (New York, 1962).

Two more general historical assessments of the era should be mentioned. F. B. Artz, *Reaction and Revolution, 1814–1832* (New York, 1934) is a general history by an historian of ideas which skillfully fits Romanticism into the events of the era. The recent study by George L. Mosse, *The Culture of Western Europe,* offers a general history of ideas of the modern period in which Romanticism is evaluated negatively.